PG2 96/7.   £9.99

THE GOOD, THE BAD AND THE MISLED

The Good, The Bad
and
The Misled

True Stories
Reflecting Different World Views
for Use in
Secondary Religious Education

MARK ROQUES
with
JIM TICKNER

MONARCH
Crowborough

First published 1994

British Library Cataloguing in Publication Data
A catalogue record for this book is available
from the British Library.

ISBN: 1 85424 258 X

Produced by Bookprint Creative Services
P. O. Box 827, BN21 3YJ, England for
MONARCH PUBLICATIONS
Broadway House, The Broadway
Crowborough, East Sussex, TN6 1HQ.
Printed in Great Britain.

This book is dedicated to
Anne Burghgraef

CONTENTS

ACKNOWLEDGMENTS

We would like to thank the following people for their inspiration and constructive critical comment. Thanks to Jonny Baker who sparked off the original idea for the book and to Jon Birch for his wonderful cover. Thanks also to Paul Alkazraji, Nik Ansell Anne Burghgraef, Janet Hunter, Richard Russell, Sue Snell and Anna Williams who have all contributed significantly to the project. Trevor Cooling and Ann Holt have read and criticised the entire manuscript; their comments have proved invaluable.

Mark would like to thank his colleagues in the Theology department at Prior Park College, Bath for their support during the writing of the book.

Mark would also like to thank his Upper Sixth Theology class for their enthusiastic response to our true stories. Thank you very much – Elaine, Dominie, Kate, Nicola, Clare, Camilla, Marianne and Jonathon. Daniel Vick and Jane Hewitt of my Lower Sixth Form group have also helped.

Lastly we would like to thank Tony Collins for his enthusiastic response to the project.

Lyric Reproduction of *'Tomorrow Belongs To Me'* by kind permission of Carlin Music Corporation, UK administrator.

Lyric Reproduction of *'Death Of A Disco Dancer'* by kind permission of Warner Chappell Music Ltd and International Music Publications Ltd.

Mark Roques & Jim Tickner
May 1994

THE USE OF STORIES IN EDUCATION

Everyone loves a good story. Children will sit enthralled for hours as long as the story is 'right'. Mischievous teenagers will terminate their playful banter and actually listen. World-weary adults will perk up and proffer a smile. A good story is always a winner.

People's lives are intriguing and alluring: the tabloid newspapers exploit our fascination with private lives, gossip and sensational revelations. How we love the 'inside story', the latest scoop. We are curious creatures, very much in love with the detail of eccentric and colourful lives.

At the same time, few of us are enchanted with the abstractions of theory and philosophy. We groan when the complexities of 'economic growth' or 'metaphysics' are mentioned. We want easy, casual entertainment. So many of us are frivolous and easily bored; we squirm when our minds are over extended.

The prophets and Jesus were only too aware of this human frailty. These imaginative communicators did not launch into long, verbose disquisitions; they did not bore the 'punters' with inaccessible treatises. They told stories. When David had successfully seduced Bathsheba, had murdered poor Uriah, how did Nathan, the prophet respond?

With great artistry and panache he told King David a yarn:

'There were two men in a certain town, one rich and the other poor. The rich man had a very large number of sheep and cattle, but the poor man had nothing except one little ewe lamb he had bought. He raised it, and it grew up with him and his children. It shared his food, drank from his cup and even slept in his arms. It was like a daughter to him.'

'Now a traveller came to the rich man, but the rich man refrained from taking one of his own sheep or cattle to prepare a meal for the traveller who had come to him. Instead, he took the ewe lamb that belonged to the poor man and prepared it for the one who had come to him.'

David burned with anger against the man and said to Nathan, 'As surely as the Lord lives, the man who did this deserves to die! He must pay for that lamb four times over, because he did such a thing and had no pity.'

Then Nathan said to David, 'You are the man!'

2 Samuel 12: 1–7

This clever and carefully constructed tale was the perfect vehicle for the communication and apprehension of truth. This cryptic story trapped David and caught him, blissfully unaware of his own wicked deeds, like a bird in a cage.

What can we learn from a story like this?

So often, in the teaching of Religious Education, we begin with such abstract concepts as 'redemption', 'eucharist', 'salvation' and 'positive discrimination'. These ideas do not endear themselves to teenagers; this point of entry into the teenager's experience is seldom successful. Perhaps we can learn something from Nathan.

Let us begin with true stories, authentic human experiences and then tease out, playfully and cryptically, the ethics, the philosophy, the religious instruction. Our point of entry can fruitfully be the humour, warmth and frailty of private lives. For example, the extraordinary story of John Newton, the slave trader turned abolitionist, is most illuminating. This tough and resourceful man spent many years of his life as a captain of a slave ship. Without doubt Newton would have participated in outrageous cruelties: the thumbscrew, the cat o' nine tails and the distribution of 'fresh food' to hungry sharks. And yet Newton ended his days as a fervent Christian, a devout abolitionist, a man who had come to understand that black people were not mere 'cargo' but fellow creatures made in the image of God.

This life of Newton can instruct us in all kinds of ways. Ethics, history, geography and religious education fuse together in an intriguing adventure story. There is so much to learn from Newton's life.

The tragic story of Hetty Green can serve as a perfect foil to Newton's life. Hetty can only be described as the world's meanest woman! Blessed with both inherited wealth and financial acumen, Hetty accrued huge sums of money and yet her deep reluctance to part with any of it made her the laughing stock of America. When her son, Ned, dislocated his knee falling off a toboggan, she refused at first to get medical attention, saying the leg would right itself. The problem refused to go away and so Hetty dressed Ned in ragged clothes and took him to the pauper's hospital. When a doctor was finally consulted, Ned's leg had become gangrenous and amputation became the only solution! When Hetty finally died in 1916 she left more than $100 million. Hardly a pauper! When Ned finally received his inheritance, he spent the money extravagantly and often wastefully.

This true story can serve many purposes. It can open up a discussion about the beliefs and convictions of two very contrasting personalities. Hetty was committed to the saving of money at almost any cost while Ned became profligate almost to the point of absurdity. Their attitudes towards money and possessions betray their deepest convictions.

A Note for Teachers

Each story can be used in at least three different ways. First, the story can simply be related and left at that – the curiosity and imagination of the pupil will be activated. Secondly, the story can be told and then clues can be suggested as to its significance. Finally, the story can be told and a detailed talk can then ensue.

In this book there are over fifty stories that will stimulate, challenge and provoke teenagers to reflect critically on their own beliefs and the beliefs of others. Each story is accompanied by appropriate 'follow -up' work which comprises suggested topics for discussion and written assignments.

This book is intended for use both by individuals and in schools. In the light of the 1988 Education Reform Act we believe that there is a real need for fresh and exciting curriculum material for students in the 14–18 year old bracket. From 1993 all schools will be inspected for the 'moral, cultural, spiritual and social development' of their children. This book encourages young people to reflect deeply about precisely these kinds of issues.

Our true stories will be our point of entry into the myriad of beliefs and commitments that shape our individual and corporate lives. We propose to deal with consumerism, fascism, nihilism, eastern religions, Orphism and gnosticism, primal religions, paganism, communism, Islam, New Age and Christianity. An unusual feature of the book will be the inclusion of seemingly non-religious ideolgies *as religion*. Consumerism and fascism require faith as much as Hinduism or Islam. Religious faith is not eliminated in such seemingly 'secular' movements; it is merely redirected. This crucial point will become clearer as our stories unfold.

It must also be mentioned that some of the stories depict the cruelty, the violence and futility of human lives. This feature of the book is unusual and controversial and some explanation is required.

First, we live in a world where almost every day we hear of murder, rape and war: our lives, all our lives, are troubled by pain and suffering. A responsible and compelling Religious Education must deal with human brokenness and human evil. This side of life cannot be glossed over and neglected.

Second, the Bible itself is extremely graphic in its depiction of human avarice, greed and lust. In Judges chapter 3 we read about the brutal assassination of a king. In the second book of Kings chapter 21 we learn of a king, Manasseh, who sacrificed his own son to a pagan god. And the details of Ezekiel chapter 23 will not even be mentioned!

Of course the inclusion of such stories must be accompanied and integrated with the lives of inspiring and virtuous men and women. Like the Bible, this book tells the stories of the good, the bad and the misled. Individual teachers will need to select carefully those stories that are appropriate for any given class.

Our first chapter will focus upon the relationship between people's beliefs and their actions, laying an important foundation for the subsequent use of our true stories.

INTRODUCTION TO BELIEFS

This book is about people and the beliefs and convictions that orchestrate their lives. Men and women can do crazy and extraordinary things. Adolf Hitler ordered his soldiers to kill six million Jews. Imelda Marcos bought three thousand pairs of shoes and, with her husband Ferdinand, stole vast sums of money from the Philippine treasury. Kim Philby, the infamous spy, was so captivated by communism that he became a double agent for the KGB and caused scores of British agents to lose their lives. Simeon the Stylite lived for thirty seven years on a sixty foot pillar and good Queen Boudicca would sometimes ritually sacrifice all her prisoners to the goddess Andraste by impaling them on stakes.

Why do people do such things? This book will attempt to give some answers to these questions.

All people live in a particular way. We are all forced to breathe, to eat, to sleep, to talk . . . to live. By being born we enter a world of choices and decisions. Today a man in Iraq has decided to torture an 'enemy' of Sadam Hussein. Today a woman in Brazil has decided to sell her body for money. Today a teenager has decided to 'sniff' cocaine. Today a woman has decided to have an abortion. Today a boy has decided to buy a gerbil. Today a teacher has decided to mark her books. It is impossible to avoid these decisions, these choices. And some of these decisions are prompted by our deepest beliefs.

1. Beliefs and Convictions

When we speak of *deep* beliefs, we are referring to the often unconscious convictions that shape and direct our lives. We can define such beliefs as powerful dispositions that guide and control the key decisions of our lives. These deep beliefs integrate and give direction to our lives.

If a woman decides to give one half of her income to the Communist Party, we enter this realm of 'conviction' or 'belief'. Again, if a man decides to become a member of the National Front we enter this realm. If a woman decides to become a nun, again we encounter profound convictions.

The key events of our lives are always earthed and grounded in these *deep beliefs* which powerfully motivate, direct and inspire. We can speak of consumerist, fascist, communist, nihilist, pagan, Hindu, Buddhist or Christian beliefs.

2. Money is Revealing

At a very simple level our deepest beliefs are revealed by our use of money. Do we hoard our cash or do we lend generously? Do we believe that our money and possessions belong ultimately to us, to the state, to our ancestors or to God? Our bank accounts will betray our true beliefs; we may claim to be concerned about poverty and yet squander and waste our money.

Some people dedicate all of their resources to the activities of gambling and drinking. There are those who purchase huge numbers of consumer-durables; there are those who give half their income to organisations like Oxfam and Christian Aid. And there are some who contribute unstintingly to the Animal Liberation Front.

Our attitudes to money reveal our commitments; a selfish attitude encourages meaness; an unselfish attitude encourages generosity. And of course there is the question of debt! Do we live so wildly that we are continually 'touching our mates for a tenner'. Without doubt there are those who lend willingly and those who borrow enthusiastically.

In all this financial activity values and beliefs weave their complex web.

3. How Do You Treat Other People?

We all relate to other people in a myriad of ways. How do we get on with our friends? Are we grumpy, cantankerous and fickle? Or are we gentle, sensitive and patient? There are those who chuckle when their colleagues at work suffer trials and tribulations and there are those who empathise with a distressed colleague.

Bullying can become a hobby for some; spite and peevish comments can dominate certain lives. There are those who are consumed with bitterness and resentment.

And there are people like Mother Teresa in the world; those who dedicate their lives to serving others. Yet again these attitudes and responses betray our deepest beliefs. We simply can't seem to escape them!

4. How Do You Treat Yourself?

We all have a relationship with ourselves. Some people can so hate themselves that they might attempt suicide. There are those who will only accept themselves if they are the correct weight; anorexia and bulimia can trouble many lives. Some people have been so convinced that their bodies are evil that they have castrated themselves! On the other hand we can find people who perceive themselves to be unbelievably wonderful and godlike. Such people never seem to be wrong and ooze confidence and self-belief. There are even those who believe that they are divine! The emperor Caligula was persuaded of his divinity and expected his Roman citizens to bow down and worship him!

It would be presumptuous and mistaken to argue that all such self-loathing or self-worship is rooted in what we have called our *deepest* beliefs and convictions. But our attitude to ourselves is rooted in a cluster of beliefs and commitments; some of these can be described as neurotic, psychotic, masochistic or self-obsessed. Nevertheless there are times when our convictions can control and direct our perception of ourselves.

5. How Do You Treat the World around You?

We all relate to the world around us. Are we indifferent to ecological issues or passionately concerned? Do we perceive animals as gods or objects to be used and abused?

The crocodile has been worshipped by some as a god. For others crocodiles are simply future handbags. In India today there are people who worship cobras; these gods must be protected and respected; they are more valuable than people! For others the cobra is simply a spitting snake that is loathed, feared and destroyed without conscience.

The ancient Celts revered and worshipped trees; the assistance of tree gods was activated by 'touching wood'. For many today trees are economic resources; nothing more, nothing less.

For some the world is neither divine nor 'inert matter'. It is a creation that must be looked after. Here again human beings cannot avoid commitments; beliefs and convictions orchestrate our response to our environment.

6. What or Who Rules the Universe?

What ultimately rules our lives? If our best friend has died in a car accident, how might we explain this tragedy? Was this death decreed by cold, impersonal fate? Perhaps a vengeful pagan goddess was responsible? In primal religions it is sometimes believed that a sorcerer or a disgruntled, dead ancestor might be to blame. The National Socialist interpretation would point to the 'eternal laws of natural selection'; nature blindly liquidates the weak and the unlucky. The Christian would refer to the painful reality of living in a fallen and broken creation. Yet again it is impossible to remain neutral about such matters. Who ultimately rules? Fate? Fickle gods? Ancestors? Natural selection? Or a loving, just God? These are some of the options that we are forced to choose.

7. What Are Your Hopes and Dreams for the Future?

For many today winning the pools and living a life of old Riley might encapsulate their personal ambition. A life of perpetual consumption and eternal leisure is the supreme goal of life.

But there are many people who would find this vision repulsive. For some the abolition of slavery became a crusade . . . a personal ambition. William Wilberforce dedicated his life to the ending of slavery; he gave his life to this task. Lenin was a man who longed and dreamed for a Communist revolution and, indeed, his dream came true in 1917!

Some Muslims expend enormous effort and energy in the realisation of Islamic theocracies; such people do not care about 'winning the pools'. And there are mystics who dream of moksha and nirvana; ascetics who long to find the bliss of 'enlightenment'. Yet again human beings cannot avoid dreams, hopes and ambitions. Our lives betray our hopes, our deepest beliefs.

8. Mix 'n' Match.

Of course life is complicated. Many people can mix conflicting perspectives into bizarre cocktails. Christians have fused their beliefs with fascist, pagan and consumerist themes. It is very easy to mix 'n' match. Ardent, committed atheists can 'touch wood' and speak of the 'lap of the gods'. The *sicarios* or hired killers of Colombia blend Catholic beliefs with pagan superstitions. There are communists who also claim to be Buddhists! Occultists who also claim to be capitalists! This syncretism can make for a complicated and perplexing world.

We will now turn to an examination of the key beliefs that motivate, guide and direct our lives. We will begin with *consumerist* beliefs.

CONSUMERISM

INTRODUCTION

For many people in Britain today, the prospect of winning the pools elicits joy and excitement. The lucky winners may well receive a cheque for £2, 000, 000; a huge fortune by any standard. There are those who might hoard this money, refusing to spend a penny and there are others who give away every penny! There are even those who fritter away their huge sum in record time.

In 1961 Keith Nicholson won £152, 319 on the pools; the cost of living in the early sixties was a fraction of today's prices – a pint of beer might have set you back ten pence! A house could be bought for five thousand pounds. Keith's wife, Vivian was delighted and when Keith received his cheque, she was asked what she planned to do. Her voice quivered with emotion as she declared . . . . 'I'm going to spend, spend, spend'.

Vivian was true to her promise and squandered the windfall on clothes, furniture, parties, alcohol and houses. Both she and her husband began to drink heavily and Keith indulged his passion for expensive cars. When Keith died in a car crash, there was not a great deal of the money left. Vivian eventually went through three husbands, several cruises and a pink Mercedes. She later wrote a book called 'Spend, Spend, Spend', which was adapted into a television play and then into a musical. She now lives in a council flat in Leeds.

This true story can serve as an introduction to consumerism. For many people in the west today, the purpose of life is to consume as many goods and services as possible. 'I shop, therefore I am' might encapsulate this way of life. But what exactly is consumerism? And what do consumerists believe? Here are some of the key beliefs of a consumerist attitude to life.

Key Beliefs of Consumerism

1. Nature as Brute Matter

Some people have believed that the world, as we normally perceive it, is nothing but a mirage! We think it is there but we are quite mistaken. It is a hologram; it is an illusion. This view may seem very odd but several of the world's most famous religions, including Buddhism, take this position very seriously.

As a consequence of this belief some people have sought very hard to *escape* from the world. Some have starved themselves to death and others have renounced all attachments to their families and possessions.

Consumerism does not embrace this belief. Consumerism, as a creed, believes that the world is very real! For many people today, the world has become a huge stockpile of raw materials that must be conquered and exploited. Forests, mountains, rivers and valleys are literally exploding with potential wealth. Kick 'nature' hard enough and she will make you a millionaire.

This attitude to 'nature' was beautifully encapsulated in the words of a North American Indian, Chief Seathl of the Suwamish tribe. He wrote these words to the President of the United States in 1855:

> We know that the white man does not understand our ways. One portion of land is the same to him as the next, for he is a stranger who comes in the night and takes from the land whatever he needs. The earth is not his brother but his enemy, and when he has conquered it, he moves on . . . . His appetite will devour the earth and leave behind only a desert.[1]

This consumerist view contrasts very strikingly with the 'hologram' view. Who would strive to conquer something that does not exist?

2. Profit Rules

The follower of the consumerist faith is convinced that profit and pleasure are the key goals of life. In the famous film *Wall Street*, the corporate raider extraordinaire, Gordon Gekko conveys this attitude with breathtaking lucidity:

Greed is good,
Greed is right,
Greed works,
Greed will save the USA.

Some religions have maintained that greed is the *source* of all the world's problems. Gekko would have no time or patience for this point of view. For Gekko man is by nature a selfish, calculating machine. Gekko is constantly wheeling and dealing; he is obsessed by one thing – profit. This man has no concern with the plight of the Amazon rainforests; nor is he concerned with the losers in life, the poor and the needy. Gekko always wants more. More money, more property, more caviar, more champagne. Enough is never enough.

3. Money Brings Happiness

The consumerist is convinced that happiness comes to those who amass vast fortunes. The richer you are the happier you are. As we have already seen, there are many people today who believe that winning the pools is a passport to everlasting bliss. When that cheque is cashed, a life of pleasure, opportunity and happiness must necessarily follow. Huge numbers of agreeable consumer-durables can be obtained at the drop of a hat: BMWs, diamonds, mansions, cruisers and swimming pools will be the order of the day.

This view contrasts strikingly with the monastic vows of 'poverty, celibacy and obedience'. There have been many people who have believed that happiness can only come to those who shun and avoid wealth.

4. You Are What You Buy

In Hitler's Germany, during the 1930's, many young members of the Hitler Youth would chant these simple words – 'You are nothing, the nation is everything'. German fascism instilled in the Geman people a profound love and respect for the 'Fatherland'. They were not important as individuals. Their identity resided in being part of the great German nation!

Consumerism instils a different type of attitude in its followers. A person's identity does not reside in a nation, a church or a community. You are what you buy! Your identity is rooted in your purchases. Consumerists are very sensitive and careful when it comes to a question of label or brand. One true story corcerns a saleman who had recently exchanged his two litre, fuel-injection Cavalier for a newer car. He was appalled to discover that his latest form of transport would be an inexpensive Maestro 1.3. Shaking with emotion, he explained to an interviewer that his wife had refused to even enter the car. 'We both sat down and wept', he said. 'We felt so ashamed!' Clearly this man and his wife had come to believe that the quality of a person's possessions defines his identity.

5. Vibrant Creativity

In order for a consumer society to thrive, it must generate high levels of consumption. As a consequence, highly sophisticated forms of advertising have developed. Television advertisements, for example, are often so captivating that they can be more interesting than the programmes which suround them.

This creative impulse helps to generate a colourful and diverse world that contrasts strikingly with the greyness and uniformity typical of communist societies.

6. *We Must Compete to Survive*

Consumerism is a profoundly individualistic way of life. It's a tough jungle out there and we're all competing for a limited number of hamburgers and personal stereos. Only the winners will survive. WATCH OUT. Dog will eat dog. Bully will eat nerd. We are all individuals in competition and only the toughest and cleverest will survive.

In a western school there is a typical response to a familiar scene. Teacher: 'A mars bar will be given to the winner of this short competition . . .' Immediately hands shoot up: 'Me sir, pick me!'

Surprisingly this is a very parochial response. In schools dominated by native North American children a totally different scenario ensues. As soon as the question has been articulated, these children group together, scrum-fashion and work the answer out together. They all want to win; they do not want anyone to lose. This cooperative response to the 'mars bar' competition contrasts very strikingly to the consumerist approach.

7. *Humans Are Things*

Consumerism, as a way of life, has a tendency to view people as commodities. In the 18th century many English people bought and sold black people as if they were items in a shop. When buying and selling becomes the sole focus of life, people can become mere 'chattels'. In Bangkok today, western people flaunt their wealth as they buy women and children for sexual servicing. Indeed it is even possible to buy a person and receive a receipt in that infamous city.

This consumerist attitude contrasts very strikingly with the biblical view of a person. In the Bible men, women and children are made in God's image. They are not things to buy and sell. They are precious and unique.

A Brief History of Consumerism

When we speak of consumerism we must be careful to distinguish between healthy consumption and 'nonsense' consumption. In a basic sense we need to consume. It is good to buy fashionable, attractive clothes. It is enjoyable and exciting to buy a new stereo. It is life-affirming to buy all kinds of goods and services. If there were no economic consumption, then our society would disintegrate; unemployment would increase enormously and the basic infrastructure of our society would collapse. But consumerism, as a way of life, does not encourage responsible and normative consumption. The belief that 'enough is never enough' undermines and corrupts healthy consumption.

Consumerism rejects the biblical convictions that 'man shall not live by bread alone but by every word that procedes from the mouth of God'. Instead the activities of buying and selling, although good in themselves, assume a distorted and destructive significance. Consumerism declares that Man shall live by bread, by beer, by cars alone. This creed rejects healthy consumption and encourages 'nonsense' consumption. A popular car sticker in California declares that 'The one with the most toys at the end, wins!' Let's now examine more closely the historical development of consumerism.

The consumerist way of life began to take a grip upon the world as early as the 1930's when this statement captured a growing change of mood:

> The purpose is to make the consumer discontented with his old fountain-pen, kitchen utensil,   bathroom or motor car, because it is old-fashioned, out of date. The technical term for this is 'obsoletism'. We no longer wait for things to wear out. We displace them with others that are not more effective but more attractive.[2]

By the next decade the idea of thrift had become even more outdated. Obsolescence was being hailed as a birthright! J.G.

Lippincott summed up the new outlook:

> The major problem is one of stimulating the urge to buy! . . . Our
> willingness . . . to part with something before it is completely worn
> out . . . . . is soundly based on our economy of abundance.[3]

A short decade later this way of life had achieved spiritual
significance:

> Our enormously productive economy . . . . demands that we make
> consumption our *way of life*, that we convert the buying and selling
> of goods into rituals, that we seek our spiritual satisfactions, in con-
> sumption. . . . . . We need things consumed, burned up, worn out,
> replaced and discarded at an ever increasing rate.[4]

What an extraordinary confession of faith! The very buying
and consumption of cars, fridges, videos, televisions and game-
systems has become both a ritual and a spiritual satisfaction.

What is the fruit of this 'ritual' in the 1990's? The lifestyle of
some Japanese people is very revealing. So important is it to
have the latest gadgetry in one's home that large numbers of
domestic appliances are *routinely thrown out in perfect working
order*. This has left the Japanese with more waste than they can
handle and their solution has been to create an island of waste in
the ocean. This 'TV Island' is now growing apace and all
manner of toxic substances are seeping from it into the
surrounding ocean.

The fate of the Dominican wine palm should cause us to
ponder. This tree produced a cherry-like fruit and wine could be
made from its juicy sap. The preferred method of extraction was
'garotting' . . . . . a form of strangulation. This, sadly, would
invariably destroy the tree. So over-exploited were the wine
palms that they became extinct in 1926. Just one among ten
thousand plant species made extinct by man in the last two
hundred years.

The appetite and greed of this modern way of life is indeed devouring the earth and leaving behind deserts and polluted seas. Perhaps Chief Seathl had a good point when he wrote his letter to President Lincoln in 1855.

All of these points will me made clearer as we look at some of our intriguing 'true stories'.

Notes

1. Quoted in Hugh McCullum and Karmel McCullum, *This Land Is Not for Sale* (Toronto: Anglican Book Centre, 1975), p.24.
2. Utne Reader* Sep/Oct 1989 p84, extracted from *Modern Publicity*, 1930.
3. *Ibid.*
4. Victor Lebow, *Journal of Retailing* (USA), 1953.

* The Utne Reader is a well-known Canadian magazine.

Elvis Presley

Elvis Presley, born in Tupelo, Mississippi in 1935 was the only child of Gladys and Vernon Presley. His mother doted on him to the point of suffocation but was to set his career in motion when she bought him a cheap guitar.

At the age of eighteen Elvis got his first job as a truck driver. With money to burn, he decided to treat his mother by cutting a record for her birthday. He was 'spotted' instantly by Marion Keisker whose persistence saw to it that Sam Phillips signed him up and he began touring Memphis. In 1955 he was 'poached' by Colonel Tom Parker who made it clear to him: 'You stay talented and sexy, I'll make amazing deals that will make us both as rich as rajas.'

He was, of course, completely right. But what was it that brought Elvis to a tragic death at the age of 42?

Certainly the death of his mother in 1958 had a harrowing effect on Elvis. Still grieving from this, he met Priscilla Beaulieu in Germany and, desperate to be loved for himself, he fell passionately in love with this young, gentle girl. Elvis worshipped this new woman in his life; she was his living doll and Elvis began to lavish gifts on her. He would buy her anything she wanted.

Yet for six months of the year he was away on tour and became an increasingly compulsive spender and lover. Huge parties would be laid on with women and drugs aplenty. He would buy and sell Cadillacs at a rate of 2 per month and once bought 300 pairs of expensive prescription sunglasses.

Elvis was beginning to feel increasingly guilty that he saw so little of his wife. This guilt prompted him to buy her an exquisite

33

horse and this led to the purchase of another horse for a friend; then one for himself, then one for each of his entourage. This was followed by cowboy outfits, a ranch and finally a fleet of trucks and trailers!

Not surprisingly Priscilla fell in love with someone willing to spend time with her and Elvis was crushed when she left him. His life sank into a debauched merry-go-round of uppers, downers, hamburgers and pizzas. Any attempt to remove his supply of drugs would enrage the 'king'; his temper had become explosive and violent. Eventually his body became so abused by his consumptive excesses that he lost control of his bodily functions and had to be wrapped in nappies. When Elvis finally succumbed to the inevitable, his bloodstream contained a total of thirteen drugs. . .

For further thought

1. Imagine that you are a teenager madly in love with Elvis. Write a letter to Elvis and tell him what you like about him.
2. You are Priscilla Presley and you have just left Elvis. Write a letter to the king and tell him why you want a divorce.
3. Do adverts encourage us to live like Elvis? Give two examples of adverts that encourage us to believe in the consumerist way of life.

Brief Notes

The life of Elvis Presley is a story of talent tragically wasted. His tendency towards compulsive buying and consuming distorted all of his relationships. Although he loved Priscilla, he also loved the permissive and hedonistic 'rock 'n' roll' lifestyle. As a committed consumerist he sought to 'buy' his wife's love. To love someone is to urge them to greater acts of consumption! Elvis could only show his affection to his wife by buying her extravagant gifts. Love, intimacy and faithfulness had become reduced to the buying of gifts. For Elvis the happiness and well-being of his wife and himself had become the art of consumption. The 'king' believed passionately that enough is never enough; both for himself and his 'living doll'. Cars, horses, mansions, drugs and hamburgers. . . this is the meaning and purpose of life.

Source: Margaret Nicholas *The World's Wealthiest Losers*, (Octopus Books, 1989).

Brazilian Street Children

Something very disturbing has been happening in recent years in the nation that brought us Pele. In this vast and heavily indebted nation millions of children have been abandoned by their impoverished parents. Forced into the cities to find food, work and accommodation, many of these children have become destitute and homeless. With little to do, they find themselves hanging around on the busy streets of cities like Rio de Janeiro. These children have become unwelcome visitors to a town that attracts many foreign tourists.

Amnesty International's B.W. Ndiaye reports that:'The death squads are again part of Brazil's daily reality. They are made up of police who torture and mutilate, knowing they enjoy almost total immunity.'

One hit-man has even left the following note on the corpse of a young nine year old girl, Patricia Hilario da Silva, which reads: 'I killed you because you didn't study and had no future.'

Why does this happen? Simply because these children hang around on streets where shopkeepers believe that they irritate and annoy wealthy tourists. What is the penalty for adversely affecting the profits of these shopkeepers? Beating, torture and often death. Poor and destitute children are worthless. In the words of one killer – 'they are lice.'

There are now 11.5 million children living in absolute poverty on Brazil's streets and Amnesty International claims that summary killing is now used as a form of population control.

For further thought

1. Imagine that you are a Brazilian street 'urchin'. You are being interviewed by a journalist. What would you say?
2. 'I killed you because you didn't study and had no future.' Discuss.
3. How can consumerism lead to the abuse of children?

Brief Notes

Poverty is so rife in Brazil that many parents do not have the resources to bring up their children and they are forced to abandon them to a life of begging. Yet these children are all too often treated like some kind of invading vermin. They are seen to have no value whatsoever. Instead they are perceived as an unprofitable 'nuisance'.

The paid-off local policemen see it as a contribution to 'national prosperity' to eliminate these 'vermin' and thereby ensure the continued influx of foreign visitors.

In the consumerist way of life there is a marked tendency to judge everything in economic terms. People are valueless if they are poor. A poor child can be cut down like a dying tree. People and trees must be destroyed in the name of prosperity. In Brazil, today, we are witnessing the fruit of a consumerist way of life: the destruction of children, forests, lakes, animals and native Indian people.

The Dumagats

Many people in the Western world would be surprised to learn that slavery is still alive and well on planet earth. According to the Anti-Slavery society there are some 200 million people today who could be described as working and living in conditions that constitute slavery. This is significantly more than when most countries abolished slavery in the second half of the nineteenth century.

In the Philippines, in hills just ninety miles east of the capital, Manila, live a tribe called the Dumagats. They survive by cutting rattan for furniture-making. They work all day long in difficult conditions for just two kilos of rice. Their owner, a *tabong* or slave master, will have inherited them in payment for a 'debt' not paid by their forefathers. The workers, themselves, earn no money. They will never be able to pay off these 'debts'. Children are thus born into slavery and whole families are available for the bargain price of 2,000 pesos (£60). The rattan they cut is made into furniture currently fashionable in the West, by factories largely staffed with under-age children. The shipments arriving in stores in New York and London represent the sweat and tears of hundreds of slave children.

For further thought

1. Why do you think that the slave trade continues to flourish?
2. You are making a film about modern slavery. What key points would you raise? How would you communicate the tragedy of this situation?
3. How is slavery related to the issue of consumerism?

Brief Notes

The widespread existence of slavery in the modern world is something that many people find hard to believe. Yet its persistent presence is strongly related to the consumerist way of life. Production and consumption are of paramount of importance, so much so that young children are routinely sold into slavery to produce goods consumed by people who have little idea of their origin. Factory and plantation owners have become the new slave traders and in their pursuit of profit are willing to accept and abuse children in payment for debts that do not really exist.

Source: Peter Lee-Wright, *Child Slaves*, (London: Earthscan Publications Ltd, 1990).

Hetty Green

Hetty Green was making $7 million a year at a time when the average American was making $490 a year. Yet talking to her could be something of an ordeal. She rarely bathed and her underclothes were never changed until they fell to pieces. Her children were never allowed to use hot water when bathing.

She moved regularly from one lodging to another, with her children in her wake. Despite amassing huge sums of money she would do anything to avoid spending it. She bought biscuits by the barrel – to cut out the grocer's profit – and lived off them for months. Her son, Ned, would be sent out with the morning papers to resell them!

On a more tragic note was her reluctance to pay doctors. After Ned had fallen from a sledge and dislocated his knee, she refused to get medical attention. She waited for the leg to heal itself but eventually had to accept that it was not going to happen. Dressing Ned in ragged clothes, she took him to the paupers' hospital in order to get free treatment. Sadly, by the time the doctor reached Ned, things were beyond repair and the leg had to be amputated.

Even after her children had left home, she tried to dominate them. In spite of this, Ned had started a colourful public career, living the high life. Sylvia, his sister, had trouble finding boyfriends; Hetty did all she could to frighten them off. Her eventual husband had to waive all rights to her property and money.

Hetty was plagued with fear that someone might attack and rob her. Visits to the bank often involved following tortuous routes, doubling back and hiding in doorways.

In 1916, after accusing a friend's housekeeper of bankrupting her employer by using full cream milk instead of skimmed milk, she had a fit of temper and burst a blood vessel. One side of her body was paralysed. Ned's response was to send for nurses and to ensure that they dressed in plain clothes. Ned knew that the thought of the expense would give his mother another stroke!

Hetty died in 1916, aged eighty, worth approximately $100 million. Ironically a great deal of it was to be dissipated by her improvident son. The effect of all the mean years was to turn Ned into a big spender. He had his chamber pots studded with diamonds, bought his mistress a $50,000 chastity belt and installed 12 pretty secretaries and a masseuse in his suite in the Waldorf-Astoria Hotel.

After Ned died in 1936, it took 200 lawyers, 385 witnesses and 4, 000, 000 words of evidence to sort out the estate.

For further thought

1. Hetty has just died and Ned has inherited all her money. What might Ned have written in his diary on that day?
2. Devise a dialogue in which Hetty Green persuades Ned to go out into the bitter winter cold and resell the newspaper she has just finished reading.
3. In what ways do **both** Hetty and Ned deviate from 'healthy' consumption?

Brief Notes

In contrast with many other consumerists, Hetty Green's passion was not to consume as many goods as possible. It was the experience of accumulating money that became her obsession. Her life was impoverished by an inability to enjoy the fruits of her own hard work. So extreme was this passion for amassing a fortune that every other aspect of her life suffered. Her personal hygiene, her nutrition, her comfort and even her children were sacrificed to her ultimate pride and joy . . . . her bank balance.

Her greed in wanting to save every possible penny led to the unnecessary amputation of her son's leg. For Hetty, 'Greed was Good', not her son's health. In common with many other consumerists she was aware of the need to compete to survive and was a formidable character in her business life. She even demanded that the bank she used should provide her with a table. This competitive drive, combined with her greed, meant that she lived in constant fear of losing her fortune and it was ironic that it was her ridiculous greed that eventually cost her her life.

Perhaps the most interesting outcome of her life was the effect she had on her son, Ned. His acts of conspicuous 'nonsense' consumption are almost unrivalled in history.

Source: Margaret Nicholas, *op. cit.*

Fouling the Nest

In his excellent book *Born to Shop*, Mike Starkey tells us about two experiences that can deepen our understanding of consumerism and its impact upon the environment.

'The holiday souvenir which has lasted me longest is not a toy donkey with salt and pepper on its back, a T-shirt or a piece of pottery. It is a large gloop of Mediterranean oil on my swimming trunks. Every time I swim it reminds me of my vacation on the sunny shores of the world's most polluted sea.

The main road near my house perenially blossoms plastic bags, tin cans, sweet wrappers and the Kentucky Fried Chicken packets which the public buy at a shop five miles away. They seem to wait till they approach my drive, throw out all the wrappers at once, and drive off chuckling into the night. Other people actually bring whole bags of rubbish out to the area of the Cambridgeshire countryside I live in and unload it all at the side of the road.

The problem of pollution is not simply one of the aesthetics – although some of us persist in the old-fashioned notion that hedges do look better without the plastic and gaudy packaging. It is a matter of the very survival of the planet.[1]

For further thought

1. Describe the consumerist attitude towards 'nature'.
2. Why have organisations like Friends of the Earth and Greenpeace become so popular in recent years?
3. You are the boss of a newly-formed recycling company. Design a brochure that will encourage people to use your service.

Notes

1. Mike Starkey, *Born to Shop* (Monarch: Eastbourne, 1989) p.149.

Imelda Marcos

Imelda Romualdez began her life in grinding poverty in the Philippines but her stunning good looks soon gained the attention of a certain Ferdinand Marcos. He realised that she would make the perfect politician's wife. After their marriage in 1954, this dynamic duo struggled together for political power. In 1965 Ferdinand became the president of the Philippines. They ruled the country with an iron fist for the next twenty one years.

Imelda soon took advantage of her position and assembled an entourage of 'ladies in waiting' to tour the world, buying and partying at will. She was a compulsive shopper and in one spree through Rome, Copenhagen and New York she spent £3 million in ninety days. Visitors to the Malacanang Palace can now inspect her unbelievable collection of 3000 pairs of shoes, 500 black brassieres, 1500 handbags, 35 racks of fur coats and 1200 designer gowns she wore but once.

Imelda had a passion for grandiose schemes; this included the infamous Manila Film Festival of 1982. As construction on the huge building to house the film festival fell behind schedule, Imelda decided that corners had to be cut; cement floors were not allowed to dry properly before the next phase of construction began. Disaster was to strike when a floor collapsed killing about 200 workers!

As the relatives arrived to claim the dead bodies, they were ordered back. Imelda had spoken – construction could not be delayed. The dead were covered in cement.

All in all it is estimated that Imelda and her husband stole something like $5 billion from the Philippines treasury.

Eventually their corrupt lifestyle was to catch up with them and in 1986 Corey Aquino was swept to power and the Marcoses were forced to flee to Hawaii.

Poor Imelda didn't have time to pack the usual 400 pieces of luggage that she would normally take. Yet, in just one piece of hand luggage, she managed to cram a wad of money, a gold, diamond-studded crown, three tiaras, a million pound emerald brooch, 60 pearl necklaces, 65 gold watches and 35 jewelled rings.

Despite all this, Imelda still believes that she is a symbol of what every Filipino would like to fight and die for:

'Freedom, justice, democracy and, above all, human dignity!'

For further thought

1. Write a sketch in which Imelda goes shopping.
2. In what sense was Imelda Marcos obsessed with 'image'?
3. You are a journalist. Your editor has asked you to write an article on the Manila Film Festival tragegy, exposing the obsessions of Mrs Marcos.

Brief Notes

The life of Imelda Marcos conveys the brutality and emptiness of extreme consumerism. Her obsession with shopping and consumption knew no bounds. Enough was never enough for this greedy and capricious woman. Imelda believed passionately that the good life would come to the eternal consumer. Her pleasure and happiness were of paramount concern to her; the happiness of her people meant very little to her as she squandered *their* money on her countless shoes.

But shopping was not her only vice. Imelda longed for glory and honour. To this end she would do anything to impress rich and powerful foreigners. It was this craving for the right 'image' that led to the death of some 200 labourers. The film festival had to be ready to impress such stars as Peter O'Toole, Susan George and Brooke Shields. For Imelda the workers had become nothing more than things. They were simply units of production that could be used and discarded in the quest to create a magnificent building. Callously, their relatives were rebuffed – with scant regard for the human dignity she claims to stand for.

This story has been more fully explored by Nigel Blundell in *Scandals* (Blitz Editions, 1992).

PAGANISM

INTRODUCTION

The cult fantasy film, *The Wicker Man*, has been acclaimed as one of the greatest horror movies of all time. A devout Christian policemen, Sergeant Howie, played by Edward Woodward, travels to the remote Scottish island of 'Summerisle' to investigate the disappearance of a young girl.

The inhabitants of the island seem very unwilling to cooperate with our hero. He is not only surprised by the lack of cooperation he receives, he becomes increasingly disturbed by the religious beliefs of all the people he encounters.

On one occasion the policeman visits the magnificent home of Lord Summerisle, the island's most important person. As he approaches the Lord's castle, he witnesses a bizarre pagan ritual – a dozen young women are dancing naked around a bonfire, pleading with the fire god for the gift of children!

Howie is shocked by this religious ceremony; Lord Summerisle is delighted and he explains to the sergeant precisely what is going on:

'Here the old gods are not dead. My father brought me up to reverence the music and the drama and the ritual of the old gods. To love nature and to fear it and to rely on it and to appease it where necessary. He brought me up. . . . '

Sergeant Howie can no longer control himself and angrily he shouts: 'He brought you up to be a pagan!'

Lord Summerisle's response to this passionate outburst is witty and urbane: 'A heathen conceivably but not, I hope, an unenlightened one.'

This dramatic scene can introduce us to the colourful and disturbing world of paganism. What was this religion that Lord Summerisle and the people of the island had returned to? The sergeant visits the local public library and he finds a book that describes the old pagan religion. This is what he found:

May day festivals. Primitive man lived and died by his harvest. The purpose of his spring ceremonies was to ensure a plentiful autumn. Relics of these fertility dramas are to be found all over Europe. In Great Britain for example, one can still see harmless versions of them danced in obscure villages on May day. . . . .

In pagan times, however, these dances were not simply picturesque jigs, they were frenzied rites ending in a sacrifice by which the dancers hoped desperately to win over the goddess of the fields. In good times they offered produce to the gods and slaughtered animals. But in bad years, when the harvest had been poor, the sacrifice was a human being. Sometimes the victim would be drowned in the sea or burnt to death in a huge sacrificial bonfire. Sometimes six swordsmen ritually beheaded the victim. The chief priest then skinned the child and wearing the still warm skin like a mantle, led the rejoicing crowd through the streets. The priest thus represented the goddess reborn and guaranteed another successful harvest next year.

Ancient Britain was profoundly pagan. Our ancestors worshipped tree gods, weather gods, sea gods and fire gods. At times this pagan religion could be brutal. In AD 60 Queen Boudicca ritually sacrificed all her prisoners by impaling them on stakes. This was done as an offering to the goddess Andraste, a direct reversion to ritual murder, in keeping with Druidic practice as described by classical authors.[1]

What are the key beliefs and practices of 'pagan' religion? We can speak of Celtic, Norse, Egyptian and Roman pagan religions. Without doubt there is regional variety and focus.

Key beliefs of Paganism

1. Nature is Divine

The ancient Egyptians worshipped cats, crocodiles, rivers, frogs and locusts. They believed that the gods took the form of particular animals and they would bow down and worship these gods. They believed that nature was divine. This belief continues to this day; in India, in the village of Deshnok in North Rajastan, hundreds of followers of the goddess Shri Karniji visit the only temple in India devoted to the worship of rats! These rats are not tame, domesticated rats; they are wild and often carry diseases.

The ancient Canaanites, for example, were addicted to the worship of nature. The Jewish king Manasseh was deeply influenced by the Canaanite pagan religion. The book of Kings tells us about his adoration of the sun and the stars:

> Manasseh bowed down to all the starry hosts and worshipped them. He built altars in the temple of the Lord, of which the Lord had said, 'In Jerusalem I will put my Name.' In both courts of the temple of the Lord, he built altars to all the starry hosts. He sacrificed his own son in the fire, practiced sorcery and divination, and consulted mediums and spiritists.
>
> 2 Kings 21:3–6

2. The Gods Are Easily Offended

The pagan gods are closely identified with nature. The Roman god, Jupiter was strongly connected to the sky and the weather. Neptune was associated with sea, water and earthquakes. Bacchus was the god of wine and Vulcan was the god of fire.

Such gods are invariably presented as fickle, egotistical and capricious. For example Mars, the god of war, is depicted as a bloodthirsty character who delights in the slaughter of men and the sacking of cities and Jupiter is more concerned with his sexual infidelities than his marriage to Juno. The Roman gods are often presented as immoral and easily offended.

Roman religion was obsessed with correct ritual. If the ritual is interrupted or the slightest mistake is made, then all must be repeated. Roman pagans were convinced that the gods would wreak havoc upon their cities if the ceremonies were not absolutely perfect! The pagan priest might well be a bloodthirsty axe-murderer but the gods would not care. Religion consisted of accurate ritual and very little besides.

It is instructive to briefly examine the cult of Bacchus, the god of wine and fertility. The orgiastic celebrations of Bacchus are known from Euripides' play *The Bacchae*. A period of fasting preceded the winter festival. Weakened by the fasting the devotees would work themselves into a frenzied dance. In this frenzy they would then eat the raw flesh with the blood in it of animals that had been torn apart.

3. Fate

Many Roman pagans believed in fate. Fate can be defined as an impersonal power that rules all of life. Fate is indifferent to human suffering and is often associated with astrology. Astrology was very popular in ancient Rome. The distinctive thought of astrology was that the movement of the planets and stars controls earthly events to the smallest detail. Venus slightly shudders and Pontius Maximus decides to divorce his wife!

The Babylonians had studied the stars very carefully and maintained careful records of their observations. Moreover they had connected the stars with religion and had developed a thorough theology based on this belief. The Babylonian gods were given an abode in the stars and identified with them. Hence Babylon was one source of the widespread star worship of the ancient world.

Astrology implied fatalism. All human affairs were governed by the stars. Free will was a figment of the imagination. One famous Roman emperor, Tiberius, was deeply influenced by this astrological fatalism and lived accordingly. Tiberius had two quite appalling 'hobbies'. He enjoyed throwing people off the cliffs by his villa in Capri; he was also a famous molester of children.

If we were to return to Rome in AD 33 and interview Tiberius, one of our questions might go like this: 'Your lordship – Why do you enjoy throwing innocent people off the cliffs at Capri?'

Tiberius might well respond, 'I can't help myself! I'm a victim of fate!'

For Tiberius, an impersonal power (fate) completely determines how we live. Women and men are not responsible for their cruel deeds; the stars twitch and people kill; the planets quiver and wars begin.

Not all pagans believed this. Many Roman citizens were convinced that the gods could cheat fate and so they would beg the gods to bring them good fortune. The ancient Roman world was divided between those who believed in capricious gods and those who believed in all-powerful fate. Who was ultimately in charge of the affairs of men? All-powerful fate or cruel gods? Pagans disagree and have disagreed about this issue.

4. Belief in Magic

Those Romans who did not believe in the all-consuming power of fate were often addicted to magic. The root idea of magic was that by employing proper means the gods could be forced to do something for you. Magic is intimately connected to manipulation. A special kind of magical document that has survived is the curse tablet. Most were written on lead and many were rolled up and pierced with a nail. Some were protected from prying eyes by the words being written backwards. The Guildhall Museum in London holds a tablet with the following curse:

I curse Tretia Maria and her life and mind and memory and

liver and lungs mixed up together, and her words, thoughts and memory; thus may she be unable to speak what things are concealed nor be able. . . . .

Very often the pagan devotee would go to a deep spring and throw the lead tablet into the water. The goddess Minerva was believed to be very appreciative of such requests; magical cursing was a regular event at the 'Roman Baths'.

There is also 'sympathetic' magic. A parallel action will produce parallel results. The Kouretes or the Salli would leap for taller crops. Temple prostitution would guarantee the fertility of the earth. Melt a wax image and your enemy would die of fever. There were also techniques to stimulate rain and thunder – bang your spear on your shield!

5. *Vows to the Gods*

Another fascinating aspect to pagan religion is the making of vows. In some situations a king might vow to kill the first person whom he sees leaving his house in return for the god's gift of military success. Others have promised to 'hold their left arm above their heads for three years' in return for the gift of a child.

One extraordinary story concerned a man who had vowed to crawl the 300 miles from Manosa to Hardwar in India – in return for the healing of his son. He promised the gods to take his two sons with him.

After one week of the journey, his younger son still weak from the illness, collapsed and died by the roadside. The man was devastated but felt unable to break his vow. Exhausted and bleeding, they continued to crawl until, just ten miles from their destination, the second son died. The father had made his promise and he would not give in; he completed his journey in sixty eight days.

6. Superstition rules

It is often not appreciated that almost all superstitious beliefs find
their origin in pagan religion. The pagan gods are addicted to correct ritual and proper procedure. Superstition is invariably trivial
and this reflects a belief in capricious and egotistical gods.

For example, the action of touching or knocking on the
nearest piece of wood is invariably associated with some
boasting or optimistic remark and is performed for fear of
offending the 'fates' and jeopardizing whatever it is that is
wished for. This practice of 'touching wood' is a relic of the
prehistoric worship of tree gods. The assistance or protection of
these gods was sought by knocking on the tree.

It is also often forgotten that the practice of launching a ship
by cracking a bottle of bubbly finds its roots in the pagan practice
of offering libations to the gods.

Indeed there are some people who are so profoundly
superstitious that life becomes an intolerable burden. All sorts of
seemingly trivial deeds are forbidden; all kinds of seemingly
unimportant actions are commanded.

Conclusion

The key theme in pagan religion is the belief in fate and the existence of egotistical, neurotic gods. Man is surrounded by spirits,
demons and gods. These supernatural beings cannot be
described as 'moral', loving or patient; they are fickle and feck-
less. They must be appeased and placated.

Notes

1. R. J. Stewart, *The Waters of the Gap.* (Ashgrove Press: Bath,
   1981) p33.

The Canaanites

When the Israelites, led by Joshua, finally entered the promised land of Canaan, they were confronted by a strange pantheon of pagan gods.

Baal, Asherah and Molech were all particularly 'high in the charts' at the time. Baal was the king and Asherah his queen. The Canaanites, whose livelihood depended on agricultural success, believed that their gods had considerable control over the weather and the crops. In other words, they were fertility gods.

In order to ensure healthy crops and large families, these gods had to be served with dedication and commitment. Any offence to the gods, no matter how minor, was liable to produce famine, plague and infant death. The main problem with these gods, from a Canaanite point of view, was their tendency to fall asleep. During the autumn and winter this wasn't too much of a worry, but in spring time they had to be awakened so that they could perform their vital role of fertilising the land.

A common ritual would be loud wailing, lasting for hours on end, beseeching the gods to rise from their slumber. If this proved ineffective then more dramatic rituals were required. This might mean that the worshippers would begin to cut their arms and legs with sharp knives. This dramatic and bloody scene would so impress the gods that they would be forced to leave their beds.

The Canaanites had also established special rooms in their temples for shrine prostitutes. Priests and worshippers could then 'visit' the temple and act out the kind of fertility activities that would strengthen and encourage the gods.

If all these rituals failed and famine and plague still threatened, then the final option would be a special ceremony to invoke Molech. The Canaanites would fill a tall, hollow metal image of Molech with hot coals until it became red hot. Then the dance would begin and a passionate pulsating rhythm would be established by the drums and more and more worshippers would work themselves up into a slashing frenzy. Then, at the right moment, young children of the tribe would be thrust into the glowing hands of Molech and die a horrible sacrificial death. The cries of the dying babies would be drowned out by the sound of the drums.

For further thought

1. Imagine that you are a Canaanite. How do you guarantee an abundant harvest?
2. How would a consumerist account of crop failure differ from that of a Canaanite follower of Baal?
3. What appeal might a fertility religion enjoy in a predominantly agricultural society?

Source: M. Roques, *Curriculum Unmasked* (Monarch: Eastbourne, 1989).

The Devadasi

Irawa had a problem. She was a girl. Her father had wanted a son and the local priest had advised him to sacrifice his daughter to the local '*devadasi*'. When Irawa was seven years of age she was taken, bathed and clothed in leaves, to the temple of the goddess Yellama. The ceremony was most dramatic. Holy men were lying down on the ground; jugs containing lively cobras were balanced precariously on their heads! Other holy men were lying in coffins made of cacti, their heads masked with mud.

Once inside the temple, Irawa had to take an oath never to marry but to have sex with any man chosen by the priest. This would usually mean the priest himself and anyone wealthy enough to bribe him handsomely. The ceremony would be completed by connecting Irawa to a statue of Yellama by means of a string of red and white beads.

Despite being banned over a decade ago, the Yellama cult still has many worshippers. The cult is based around the story of a sage who ordered his son to chop off his mother's head as punishment for her unchaste thoughts. The son then brought her back to life by attaching his mother's corpse to the head of an untouchable woman. . . . . . . Yellama.

Irawa has now decided to abandon this degrading practice of religious prostitution.

'It's a terrible life' she says. 'The men abuse me because I will not sleep with them anymore and they're trying to get my parents to force me to leave the village.' It is not uncommon for the priests to arrange for the girls to be sent to the brothels of Bombay, Madras and Delhi.

The government has been working hard to curb the practice

but it still continues. At a recent full moon celebration over 2000 girls were initiated as 'devadasi' or shrine prostitutes. State interference iş not well received by the priests and farmers who believe that Yellama must be appeased in order for rain to fall, crops to grow, and sons to be sired. This has even led to the killing of two police officers who recently attempted to break up a ceremony.

The priests are also angry at the government's decision to strip them of their treasures. These tributes of cattle, gold and money have increased greatly over the past 500 years. Perhaps not surprisingly, no donations are ever passed on to the Yellama prostitutes who, once they are old and gnawed by disease, wander the countryside with their hair long and matted, begging for alms.

For further thought

1. Why do the followers of Yellama practice shrine prostitution?
2. What is sympathetic magic? Give examples.
3. Devise an imaginary dialogue between a policeman who is attempting to rescue a young girl from a life of shrine prostitution and a priest of Yellama.

Brief Notes

This unusual story highlights an intriguing conflict between a pagan and a secular worldview. The followers of Yellama believe in capricious gods and goddesses. These gods must be appeased and placated with sympathetic magic and sacrifice. Failure to please the gods will incur the wrath of Yellama and a poor harvest. This religion is very similar to Celtic and Canaanite fertility religions.

The two policemen, on the other hand, do not share these beliefs. They are employed by a secular government. Fertility or infertility is a purely natural occurence; it has nothing to do with unseen gods or spirits. Their opposition to shrine prostitution leads to their murder!

Source: *The Independent*, Wednesday 6 February 1991.

Montezuma II

By the time Christopher Columbus landed on the shores of the Americas in 1492, an impressive civilisation, dominated by a tribe known as the Aztecs, had established itself in the area now known as Mexico. The future rulers of this proud people were always carefully groomed and even as the Spaniards were sailing ashore, a small child named Montezuma II was receiving a special education to prepare him for his future role as king.

This education consisted largely of religious training in such things as fasting, prayer and cutting and piercing his own flesh. He learned to read Aztec picture-writing and grasped the complexities of the Aztec calendar. As he grew older he became a 'Master of Cuts', an experienced warrior and mastered the vital skill of capturing his enemies alive in battle.

When Montezuma II's uncle died in 1503, he ascended to the throne and became emperor of a vast empire stretching from the Pacific to the Atlantic. The wealth of the Aztecs was constantly growing as a result of the tributes they exacted from conquered tribes and Aztec nobles lived in great luxury. Yet even the nobles trembled before Montezuma II, who in their eyes was nothing short of a god.

Despite all this, Montezuma II lived in constant fear and dread. The Aztec religion was one of deep fatalism and Montezuma II was alert to all kinds of signs of impending doom. A comet flying across the sky, unexpected floods, temple fires and reports of strange, light-skinned, bearded men arriving in the east were all signs to be watched closely. Montezuma II was all too aware that one of his gods, Quetzalcoatl, was pale and bearded, and was due to return from the east.

Indeed the news became even more alarming when he heard of their snorting, thundering beasts and deadly 'fire sticks'. When the Spaniards began to march on their capital city, Tenochtitlan, an island settlement replete with many temples to their gods, Montezuma II offered to pay them a tribute.

However, to give the Spaniards a sniff of gold was a fatal mistake and Montezuma II decided to arrange an ambush. This went badly wrong, largely because the Aztec warriors tried very hard not to kill any of the Spaniards. Instead they wanted to capture them so that they could be used for human sacrifice. These sacrifices were vital to keep the sun-god, Huitzilopochtli, happy. The sun-god was believed to need human hearts to feed on and, if a plentiful supply was not forthcoming, then the sun would simply disappear.

The Spaniards advanced upon Tenochtitlan and Montezuma II denied any involvement in the ambush; reluctantly he agreed to become a vassal of Spain. However his war-like people were not supportive of this policy and when he appeared before them, they showered him with stones and spears. The Spaniards claimed that he died under this hail of weapons but it is possible that they took the opportunity to murder him.

Montezuma had been in power for sixteen years when his reign was cut short by the Spaniards. The Europeans then began what was to become a systematic destruction of the Aztec culture.

Source: N. Harris, *Life & Times: Montezuma and the Aztecs* (Wayland Publishing: 1985).

For further thought

1. What is 'fate'? How did the Aztec belief in fate render them vulnerable to the Spanish soldiers?
2. Why did the Aztecs prefer to capture their enemies alive in battle?

3. What aspects of Aztec life were important in the education of a future king?

Brief Notes

Paganism is often associated with the worship of nature. In some pagan cultures, the sun can become an object of worship; this can sometimes lead to the practice of human sacrifice.

The Fisherman's Friend

In our modern technological world, there are many who take great pleasure in mocking superstitious behaviour. Despite this, our pagan past continues to exert a powerful influence upon many. Newspapers are filled with horoscopes. It has been reported that Americans spend in excess of $125 million per year on various forms of fortune-telling and divination and the Duke of Edinburgh has admitted that he always gives his polo helmet seven taps for luck before beginning a game!

One fascinating example of superstitious behaviour revolves around a Yorkshireman named Arnie West who regularly spends his holidays in Scarborough. Whenever Arnie visits any of the pubs or ale-houses on the seafront, he can clear them quicker than an irate landlord. What could be the reason for this remarkable lack of popularity? Well, it turns out that he is believed to bring bad luck to the local fishermen.

Arnie, an undertaker, can put the 'jinx' on any fishing trip. He has been blamed for storms, mists and a host of other disasters. As Albert Fishburn, fishing-boat owner, comments: 'We have lost crab pots, we have had engine trouble, cables have snapped and we have had poor catches. And a man once fell overboard when he stepped back to talk to Arnie on the dockside.'

Poor old Arnie is considered so unlucky that few landlords can afford to entertain him. Regularly he is asked to vacate the local public houses, leaving a bevy of quaking fishermen in his wake. As landlord James Haig confirmed, 'The fishermen tell incredible hard-luck stories after seeing Arnie. I'm afraid I'd have to turn him away if he called for a drink.'

Arnie himself laughs it all off, and puts it down to the

superstitious nature of fishermen. As he comments ruefully, 'They blame me for everthing that goes wrong. I can empty a pub full of fishermen quicker than anyone. But I am really the fishermen's friend.'

For further thought

1. How is superstitious behaviour related to our pagan past?
2. Give three examples of superstitious behaviour. Explain how these examples are connected to pagan beliefs.
3. How does superstition activate fear in many peoples' lives?

Source: *The Sunday Mirror,* 2nd June 1974.

Caligula

During the reign of the Roman emperor Tiberius, a young child called Gaius would often be taken by his father on army campaigns. He swiftly became something of a lucky mascot and would be dressed up in a uniform that included hand-made boots known as 'caligae'. The old soldiers soon began to dub him Caligula and the name stuck.

During his teenage years, Caligula displayed a tendency towards extravagance and sexual adventure. When Tiberius appointed him as his heir at the age of 25, it was hoped that he would grow out of these habits. In fact, quite the opposite was to occur.

Caligula began his reign with generous tax rebates and further strained the treasury by establishing lavish circuses in Rome. These were no ordinary circuses. They consisted largely of a collection of lions, elephants, bears and panthers. These poor creatures were hunted down in the arena and bloodily despatched. . . . .to the delight of the spectators.

Gladiators and charioteers were enticed to fight to the death for large cash prizes and the shows became hugely popular. The fact that the Emperor had forced his three sisters to sleep with him was conveniently forgotten.

After a year of his reign, Caligula fell ill and the circuses were stopped. Romans gathered in their thousands to beseech their gods to save the Emperor. Within a month the fever had broken and the Emperor declared, 'I wasn't really ill, I was just being reborn as a god."

The circuses began again, in even more extravagant fashion. Soon the expense began to tell and the shows started to feature pathetic and unimpressive animals. On one occasion some citizens even began booing the Emperor. Enraged, the Emperor had them seized and fed to the starving creatures. This gave him an idea that would save money. Rome's jails were slowly emptied as fresh animal meat was replaced by fresh human meat as a way of feeding the circus animals.

Caligula's liking for animals was even extended to installing them in office. Incitatus, his favourite horse, was promoted from Senator to Consul of the Roman Empire, in celebration of the Emperor's achievement of 'marching' across the Bay of Naples via 4000 connected ships.

Unfortunately, that night, a storm wrecked half the ships riding at anchor and Caligula swore revenge on Neptune, god of the sea. This he gained when camped in Boulogne, during one of his foreign campaigns. Lining up his soldiers along the beach, Caligula rode into the water and took to it with his sword. Slashing at the waves, he ordered the catapults to fire, followed by the archers. The offensive was rounded off with an infantry charge. As the soldiers left the sea they were commanded to loot it by removing piles of sea shells.

Returning to Rome in triumphant mood, Caligula was unaware of the growing conspiracy to remove him. Indeed he made plans to decapitate every statue of the gods in Rome and replace the removed head with a model of his own. But Caligula's cruelty finally caught up with him when Colonel Cassius Chaerea of the Imperial Guard stabbed him to death.

For further thought

1. You are Colonel Cassius Chaerea. You have decided to assassinate Caligula. Why have you decided to kill the emperor?
2. Imagine that you are a Christian living during Caligula's reign. Why would you be reluctant to worship the emperor?
3. Caligula boldly declared himself to be a god. In what ways did his life reflect the fickle nature of the Roman gods?

Brief Notes

Emperor worhip was an important feature of Roman pagan society. Many Christians refused to worship emperors like Caligula and they were severely persecuted for this 'crime' against the emperor. The early Christians believed that it was idolatrous to worship a Roman emperor.

Source: *Crooks, Crime and Corruption*. (London: Chancellor Press, 1987).

FASCISM

INTRODUCTION

There is a dramatic scene in the famous film *Cabaret* where a young blond boy sings a rousing and poignant song. German men and women are quietly enjoying a beautiful summer's day as they sip their wine and beer in the garden of a German 'bierkeller'. The song arouses them from their inactivity and as the song comes to its climax, the entire tavern is standing proudly, their arms outstretched in joyful salute. Here are the words to that inspiring song.

The sun on the meadow is summery warm
The stag in the forest runs free
But gathered together to greet the storm
Tomorrow belongs to me

The branch of the linden is leafy and green
The Rhine gives its gold to the sea
But somewhere a glory awaits unseen
Tomorrow belongs to me

The babe in his cradle is closing his eyes
The blossom embraces the bee
But soon there's a whisper of arise arise
Tomorrow belongs to me

Oh Fatherland, Fatherland

show us a sign
Your children have waited to see
The morning will come when the world is mine
Tomorrow belongs
Tomorrow belongs
Tomorrow belongs to me

This song can help us to understand the colourful and shocking world of fascism. The song is filled with hope and expectation. The sun, the stag and the branch of the linden tree remind us of a world that knows no pain. The baby is sleeping softly in his cradle and the Rhine is filled with gold. What a happy world!

And yet we sense something rather menacing and macabre. 'The morning will come when the world is mine' sings our handsome, blue-eyed soldier boy. Tomorrow belongs to me.

Precisely who will own this world, we might ask? The answer to this disturbing question is immediately answered by the very next scene in the film. Fritz is madly in love with a beautiful woman, Natalia, and he begs her to marry him. She declines his imploring request and drives away in her expensive motor car. Fritz sprints after and she brings the car to a halt. Desperately he pleads with her, 'Why won't you marry me?'

'Don't you see what is happening in Germany today?' she says, 'I am a Jew. You are not.' And so Natalia drives away, tearful and sad. As a Jewish woman, Natalia does not belong; her race is inappropriate!

The Nazis believed that only the racially pure would inherit this future paradise of summery scenes and golden rivers. Jews, gypsies, blacks and the mentally-handicapped would be elimated; such *Untermenschen* or sub-humans would be destroyed.

By 1939 the Nazi party had sterilised approximately 375,000 people: some 200,000 feeble-minded, 73,000 schizophrenics, 57,000 epiletics and nearly 30,000 alcoholics. In 1942 Hitler initiated his mass extermination programme of Jews, gypsies and other 'racially undesirable elements'. It is estimated that the Nazi regime murdered some six million Jewish men, women and children.

What did the Nazis believe about the meaning and purpose of life? What were their deepest convictions? Why did they torture and kill so many people? For many the Nazi mentality seems to be completely incoherent and irrational; a group of hooligans spoiling for a fight. But there is much more to it than this. National Socialism (Nazi for short) is a particular type of fascism and it is well worth examining this most aggressive and virulent movement.

Key Beliefs of Nazism

1. All of Life on Earth is a Struggle for Survival

The Nazi movement was very influenced by the ideas of Social Darwinism. Hitler, himself, was very impressed by this philosophy that had become popular in Europe at the end of the 19th century. Evolution, according to this perspective, was cruel and merciless. Life is in essence a ruthless struggle for existence. Insects, animals and human beings are all involved in a titanic struggle for survival. Every creature is constantly at war with its 'neighbour'. According to Social Darwinism, humanitarian efforts to protect the weak and vulnerable members of society contradict the basic nature of human life. Social and political policy must adapt itself to this fundamental principle.

In a speech to officer cadets in 1944, Hitler made this point very clearly:

> Victory is to the strong and the weak must go to the wall. She (Nature) teaches us that what may seem cruel to us, because it affects us personally or because we have been brought up in ignorance of her laws, is nevertheless often essential if a higher way of life is to be attained. Nature . . . . . knows nothing of the notion of

humanitarianism which signifies that the weak must at all costs be surrounded and preserved even at the expense of the strong.[1]

2. *Man is a Beast of Prey*

We now turn to the Nazi view of a person. If nature is cruel and violent this leads to the belief that man, himself, is a beast of prey. He is a predator, a tiger whose main mission in life is to kill and eat weaker animals. A tiger feels no compassion for the deer it has suddenly pounced upon. Indeed a tiger who felt compassion for Bambi the deer would not be a tiger at all! Merciful, sensitive tigers would not be able to survive.

Hitler wanted to create a new generation of cruel children! On one occasion he remarked to a friend that:

> My system of education is a harsh one. Weakness must be stamped out. The world will shrink in trepidation from the youngsters who grow up in my Ordensburgen. A violent, masterful, dauntless, cruel younger generation—that is my aim. There must be nothing weak and tender about it. Its eyes must glow once more with the freedom and splendour of the beast of prey.[2]

Hitler believed that there were two kinds of people: the hunters, those who rule, dominate and kill; and the hunted, those who are weak, pathetic and 'ripe for destruction'.

3. *Compassion is Sinful*

National Socialism redefines morality. For many people in the world today kindness, love and compassion are virtues that should be encouraged. Most of us want friends who are loving and compassionate. Not so the Nazi. Nazi propaganda films argued that attitudes of love, compassion and pity were *unnatural and sinful*. To be cruel is to affirm the cruelty and violence of nature. By contrast pity and compassion thwart and frustrate the process of evolution.

Nazi propaganda films would show pictures of doctors caring

for physically-handicapped people and comment critically, 'In the last few decades mankind has sinned terribly against the law of natural selection. We have allowed the weak to live'.[3]

The Nazi believed in the concept of sin! And yet sin had nothing to do with the rejection of God's law. Sin was understood as the turning away from the cruelty of nature and evolution!

The Nazi spoke of a 'higher' morality that would reject the morality of 'pity' and compassion.

4. The History of the World is the Struggle of Race

Communists, as we will see, identify history with the class struggle, while the Nazis were convinced that race struggle was the key impulse of history. Just as strong animal races would emerge triumphant from the process of evolution, the best *blood* had to prevail in the competition between human races and the best blood was to be found in the 'Aryan' race. The Nazis referred to all nordic peoples (Scandinavian, British and German etc) as Aryan; there is some mystery as to the origin of this term but the meaning is quite clear. Blond, blue-eyed Germans and Norwegians have good blood – they are Aryan. Jewish and black people have bad blood – they belong to inferior, non-Aryan races.

The Nazis believed passionately that throughout the world there existed an incredible struggle between Aryan and non-Aryan races. The key non-Aryan race, and the most to be despised, was the Jewish race. Hitler believed that the Jew was a parasite; a leech who survived by sucking other creatures' good blood. The Nazi believed that the Jew was a worthless, lazy creature who in evolutionary terms was 'ripe for destruction'. Natural selection had decided to eliminate the Jew.

5. Solution – Eliminate All Jews and Other Undesirables

Nazi thinkers proposed a radical solution to the 'sin' of the world. Inferior racial groups would be exterminated; this would include Jews, blacks, and gypsies. The mentally-handicapped, the physically-handicapped, homosexuals, alcoholics and 'unproductives' would also be 'dispatched' by the Aryan super-men.

Hitler did not intend to exterminate *all* inferior races. Slavic people would become a 'slave class'. These 'sub-humans' would toil relentlessly in the factories and farms of the 'Fatherland' ; they would bring beer and 'Wurst' to their masters and mistresses. These slavic sub-humans would be genetically bred to be obedient, docile and slave-like.

6. A Totalitarian State is Required

The Nazi despised democracy. Democracy embraces the belief that governments should be replaced periodically; every four or five years the 'people' should be allowed to choose a new gov-ernment. Nazis argued that democracy was opposed to all proper Nazi values. Weak, stupid people should not be allowed any say in the affairs of the state. Strong, virile 'Führer personalities' must rule the masses.

The Nazi state is totalitarian. This means that the government should take control of all areas of life. Banks, business companies, schools, universities etc must be controlled by virile 'Führer personalities'. Political opposition to the Nazi party must be eliminated.

For the Nazi, the individual has no great significance. He or she is expendable if he or she threatens any aspect of the national life. The Hitler Youth encapsulated this Nazi conviction when they chanted the following slogan: 'Du bist nichts, das Volk ist alles.' (You are nothing, the people are everything). Unlike consumerism, Nazism is anti-individualist. The aim of life is to further the glory and power of the German nation. Shopping and consumption are not important!

7. National Socialism – A Pseudo-Religion?

Many writers have argued that National Socialism is a pseudo-religion (false religion). Hitler often spoke of himself as a sav-iour or messiah. He once declared, 'That you have found me and that you have believed in me, this is what has given your life a new meaning, a new task.'[4]

Hitler called for faith, hope and obedience. It was almost as if he believed that he was the 'Light of the World'. His destiny was to take the Aryan people into the promised land – a land of milk and honey, a land where leeches and sub-humans would not exist.

It is intriguing that German schoolchildren were even taught to pray to the Führer! The following prayer was devised for children in Cologne.

Führer, my Führer, given to me by the Lord,
Protect and preserve me as long as I live!
You have saved Germany from its deepest distress.
Today I thank you for my daily bread.
Stay with me for a long time, don't leave me.
Führer, my Führer, my faith and my light!
Hail to you, my Führer![5]

National Socialism can be described as a specific type of fascism. It is highly developed and, given its basic assumptions, is coherent and convincing. Fascism, in its broadest sense, is obsessed with two fundamental concepts – *struggle and race*. Whenever a racial group seeks to destroy another racial group we can speak of 'fascism'.

Consumerism, as a creed, emphasises the struggle of the individual to master his environment. Fascism rejects this individualism. Man is not a solitary predator! He hunts always in a pack and that pack is defined by race and blood.

In the world today there is a tremendous resurgence of neo-fascism. In the former Yugoslavia Serbs are 'ethnically cleansing' particular areas of all Croat and Muslim peoples. Fascist and neo-nazi groups are becoming increasingly popular throughout Europe. Hitler's infamous book *Mein Kampf* has been experiencing a revival!

Notes

1. Institut fur Zeitgeschichte, Hitler's speech to officer cadets at the Bergof, 22 June, 1944.
2. H. Raushning, *Hitler Speaks*, (Butterworth, 1939) p247.
3. As shown on 'Selling Murder' *Without Walls*, Channel 4.
4. H. Raushning, *op. cit.* p145.
5. As quoted in *The Church in the Twentieth Century* (Vol 7) by L. Praamsma (St. Catherines, Ontario, Canada: Paidea Press, 1981).

Adolf Hitler

Perhaps contrary to expectations, the young Adolf Hitler was no romper-stomper in hob-nail boots. He was, in fact, a studious and unexceptional boy given to prolonged day-dreaming.

His father, Alois Hitler, was an Austrian of strict, conservative, middle-class stock; proud of his own achievements, but largely uninterested in the youthful activities of his son. When Adolf was 14, his father died and the family moved from Braumau-am-Inn to Linz, where they survived on a government pension.

It was during this period that Adolf decided that he would become a painter. Despite his limited talent with the brush, he was determined to pursue a creative career. At the age of 18 he moved to Vienna and took the entrance exam for the Vienna Academy of Arts. His lack of artistic ability was dramatically exposed when he failed to gain entry to the academy.

Disconsolate, Adolf was further rocked by the death of his mother in 1908. Adolf, who adored his mother, was heartbroken but his spirits were lifted by the news that he was to receive a healthy inheritance. Unsure of himself, the young Adolf adopted a casual and bohemian lifestyle. He would spend many hours sitting in cafés discussing politics and philosophy into the early hours of the morning.

In 1912 his money ran out and an embittered Adolf took a job on a building site. With few close friends, he gradually began to develop an intense hatred of anyone he perceived as an outsider. Later in his life, this hatred would develop to horrific expression. After a year or so, Adolf moved to Munich and followed with interest the developing conflicts in Europe.

When World War I broke out in 1914, he joined a Bavarian infantry regiment and was keen to prove his commitment to the nation he loved. As a company runner, he dodged bullets with remarkable dexterity and was decorated twice for his courage. Eventually he was struck down by the dreaded mustard gas and before he could recover the war was over.

After leaving hospital, Hitler joined the German Workers' Party. Rapidly he rose up the hierarchy of the party and assumed a leading role, changing the name of the party to the National Socialist German Workers' Party. He adopted the swastika emblem and became increasingly aware of his gift for oratory. Hitler perceived that he could capture the attention of any audience, large or small. His ability to engage people and manipulate their thinking had an almost hypnotic quality. With such gifts he became a prominent political figure and united many right-wing groups behind him. In 1933 he became Reich Chancellor of the German nation.

Hitler's reign of terror began in earnest. Promptly, he established a loyal army, the SA, whose very presence was enough to intimidate the hard-pressed citizens of Germany. Hitler, though, was no fool and being aware of the parlous state of the German economy he called in his financial wizard, Hjalmar Schacht. In the space of three years, he effected an economic miracle, and reduced unemployment from around six million to a few hundred thousand.

Buoyed by this success, Hitler accelerated the rearmament of Germany, contemptuously breaking the Treaties of Versailles and Locarno. In 1939 he invaded Poland, initiating World War II, and wasted no time in occupying Denmark, Norway, Holland, Belgium, Luxembourg and France in 1940. In 1941 he added Yugoslavia and Greece to his military conquests and completed his stranglehold over the European mainland.

From the very beginning of his life in power, Hitler ordered the construction of his infamous concentration camps. Initially it was his political rivals that were dispatched to these brutal regimes, but Hitler was quick to move on to other groups that he labelled 'useless eaters'. In 1939, for instance, he signed an order for the murder of 100,000 invalids, including some 3,000 children from special schools. After a strong complaint from the church, Hitler began to target other groups. The Gypsies became the next 'useless eaters' to suffer at the hands of Hitler; 500,000 of them were killed. The Polish ruling classes also faced extermination and about one million people suffered death. However, as we all know, Hitler reserved his greatest ferocity for the Jews. An unrelenting attack resulted in a death toll in the region of four to six million people. This genocidal fury was only halted when the allied armies defeated the German forces in 1945. Hitler committed suicide shortly before he would have been captured.

Tragically Hitler had been allowed to live out the perspective he had outlined in his infamous book, *Mein Kampf.*

> What we must fight for is to safeguard the existence and reproduction of our race and our people, the sustenance of our children and the purity of our blood, the freedom and independence of the Fatherland, so that our people may mature for the fulfilment of the mission allotted it by the Creator of the universe.

For further thought

1. What did Hitler mean by the expression 'useless eaters'?
2. Why did Hitler believe that 'victory is to the strong and the weak must go to the wall'? (See section 1 in this chapter.)
3. What do Nazis mean by the 'eternal laws of natural selection'? (See section 3 in this chapter.)

Source – *Crooks, Crime and Corruption.* No single author. (London: Chancellor Press, 1987).

Kolbe

The brutality of life in the Nazi death-camps was never more powerfully illustrated than in the story of Maxmilian Kolbe.

Kolbe, a Polish Catholic Priest, had been arrested in 1941 for helping Jewish refugees and was sent to Auschwitz. The treatment of human beings he was to witness was truly horrific: torture, floggings, disease, starvation and, of course, the gas chambers. Yet Kolbe reacted by reaching out to his fellow prisoners, sharing food, comforting them and holding religious services.

It was in July of 1941 that Kolbe astonished his fellow prisoners. There had been an escape from the camp and the Nazis exacted revenge by choosing ten men to starve in an underground bunker. One of the chosen men was so distraught by his selection that he cried out, 'Oh my poor wife, my poor children, I shall never see them again.'

To the surprise of all the other prisoners, Kolbe stepped forward and offered himself in the man's place. Incredibly the Gestapo officer in charge, Karl Fritzsch, actually spoke to him (Nazis would not normally enter into conversation with 'sub-humans').

'Who are you?' asked Fritzsch.
'A Catholic priest,' responded Kolbe.

All present were amazed when Fritzsch gestured to the reprieved man to return to his place.

The ten condemned men were taken to an airless bunker with no food. According to an eye-witness they prayed fervently.

When the doors were opened, some begged for bread but instead were shot or beaten. Kolbe never begged but raised the spirits of the others. Eventually only Father Kolbe was left and the Germans grew impatient. They needed the cell for a new batch of 'sub-humans'; Kolbe was taking far too long to die!

Exasperated and bemused, they sent in the head of the camp hospital, a German criminal named Bock, to administer a lethal injection of carbolic acid. Kolbe gave his arm to the executioner and died with a prayer on his lips.

For further thought

1. Why did the Nazis want to eliminate all Jewish people?
2. Why were the other prisoners so surprised when Karl Fritzsch accepted Kolbe's bargain?
3. How have Darwinian ideas influenced the Nazi movement?

Source: Mary Craig, *Candles in the Dark* (Hodder and Stoughton: London, 1984).

Ethnic Cleansing

'Ethnic cleansing' has come to symbolise one of the greatest tragedies of the early 1990's. These words, which readily elicit shudders of horror, refer to the mass genocide of many Croats and Muslims by Serbians in Bosnia, a large section of former Yugoslavia. The concept of 'ethnic cleansing', however, is not of recent origin. It dates back to the second world war when Serbians and Muslims were being 'cleansed' by the Croats in cooperation with the Nazis.

This 'cleansing' took place in concentration camps throughout Yugoslavia in which non-Croats, who had been driven from their homes, were placed. One such misfortunate was Branko Jungic, a young Serbian who met his death by systematic mutilation in a concentration camp known as Jasenovac. He was beheaded by a large saw and photographed for posterity. Unfortunately, he was only one of the 700,000 men, women and children who were slaughtered in Jasenovac alone. As in the other concentration camps, people did not die in gas chambers but were killed by individual acts of savagery. Thousands were hung from mass gallows, butchered by saws, axes and other instruments of torture or thrown into rivers with blocks of concrete tied to their waists. Women often suffered the humiliation of being gang-raped and mutilated in grotesque fashion. Official documentation and photographs testify to the unspeakable horror of this reign of terror.

Years later it was discovered, through Croatian military records found in a former Austro-Hungarian army barracks, that this systematic process of capturing land and executing non-Croats was officially referred to as 'cleansing'. It was the horrific and almost inevitable outcome of the merging of the Nazi doctrine of contempt for *Untermenschen*, otherwise known as subhumans, with ethnic hatred. Sadly, fifty years later 'ethnic cleansing' has again become a reality. This time it is the Serbians who are the principal aggressors. They are acquiring land and homes by informing their non-Serbian residents and owners that it no longer belongs to them. Anyone daring to oppose this process risks being 'cleansed'.

For further reflection

1. What is 'ethnic cleansing'? In what sense can we describe this practice as 'fascist'?
2. What is meant by the Nazi term – *Untermensch*?
3. In what ways does the conflict in the former Yugoslavia reflect Nazi preoccupations?

Source: Article by R Fisk in *The Independent* (15 August 1992).

Nasreen

Nasreen is a sixteen year old Pakistani girl who lives in the east-end of London. Her mother spends most of her time beside the window of her bedroom with a ready supply of anti-depressants and sleeping tablets.

They are a family under siege. Virtually every day and night they are tormented by fascist and racist groups. Nasreen graphically describes their behaviour: 'They go in circles, they go round and round. Or maybe they just sit, and do nothing at all. Or maybe they just hit the door or just throw rocks.'

Shortly after they had moved into the house, they were attacked by a gang of forty people, who threw stones, smashed the shop windows and daubed swastikas all over the house. Amid the attack they gave Nazi salutes and demanded 'f**king Pakis out'. This lasted for six hours.

Repeated phones calls to the local police force were to no avail. Not a single police officer turned up. Their attitude often seems to be that the offenders are juveniles and therefore too difficult to prosecute.

Nasreen has tried writing to her M.P. and to the Prime Minister, but all these efforts have fallen on stony ground.

Nasreen's family is just one among many that are persecuted by members of fascist groups on an almost daily basis. Tragically the Home Office estimates that Asians are fifty times more likely to be attacked than white people.

For further thought

1. Imagine that you are Nasreen. The local boot-boys have

arrived to torment you and your family. What might you write in your diary?
2. Construct a dialogue between Nasreen and her mother.
3. Imagine that you are Nasreen. Write a letter to your M.P. telling him or her about your plight.

Source: J. Pilger, *Heroes* (Pan Books: London, 1986).

No Surrender

Many Japanese have a traditional belief that they are the direct descendents of the sun-goddess Amaterasu-Omi-Kami. Such descent destines them to be the supreme people of the world. The World War II soldiers of the Imperial Japanese Army were totally dedicated to their nation; to these brave and resilient men, duty to Japan and their divine emperor was paramount. Capture was an unthinkable disgrace and to avoid such a humiliation Japanese soldiers would often take their own lives.

Indeed the famous Kamikaze pilots actually gave their lives by flying their planes directly into American warships. Packed with explosives, these planes could cause untold damage.

One amazing tale revolves around a soldier named Ito Masashi. In October 1944 he survived an ambush with Corporal Iroki Minikawa. Existing on grubs and roots, they avoided capture and developed their own language of clicks and signs. After eight years of this spartan existence, they stumbled across the rubbish dump of an American airbase and raided it regularly for supplies.

The worst aspect of their existence was the rainy season which lasted for two months. They would sit in their hiding-place eating berries and frogs. The two of them were convinced that the war was not over; the emperor had pulled out the troops for tactical reasons. They ignored the leaflets dropped on the island explaining the surrender of Japan. This was an American trick!

After sixteen years of hiding and surviving they were finally captured by American Marines. It took many months in captivity to convince Masashi that the war was over.

For further thought

1. How was Japanese nationalism related to traditional Japanese
    religious beliefs?
2.° Tell the story of Ito Masashi.
3. Design a leaflet which attempts to persuade Japanese soldiers
    to surrender.

Brief Notes

This Japanese obsession with the supremacy of their nation had a
decidedly fascist ring to it. This belief in the superiority of the
Japanese race was intimately connected to the goddess Amaterasu-Omi-Kami.

Source: N. Blundell, *Bizarre & Eccentric* (Amazon Publishing,
          1992).

EASTERN RELIGIONS

INTRODUCTION

In this chapter on eastern religions we will examine both Hinduism and Buddhism. We will begin with Hinduism.

Rabi was a young Hindu who was born into the Brahmin caste. Amazingly his father never once spoke to him during their short time together. For eight long years Rabi had longed for some kind of communication with his dad. And yet it never came.

Shortly after his marriage, his father had left the family home and began to meditate in a local temple. For eight long years he did not utter a single word to anyone. Rabi's mother would come every day to the temple to wash, feed and clean her husband. The normal activities of life – eating, drinking and going to the toilet – had been abandoned.

When Rabi asked his mother why his dad would not speak, she explained to him: 'Your father is someone special – the greatest man you could have for a father. He is seeking the true self that lies within us all, the One Being, of which there is no other. And that's what you are too, Rabi.'[1]

Rabi had mixed feelings about his father's exalted position: 'Though I accepted the idea that a higher choice caused my father never to speak to me, his only child, I could not deny the gnawing emptiness, the intense longing, the peculiarly uncomfortable hunger that I learned to live with, even to ignore, but never conquered.'[2]

Rabi's father was so consumed by his trance-like state that he never acknowledged any human presence even though many admirers came from miles around to worship him and to lay before him their offerings of fruit, flowers, cotton cloth and money. With reverence and awe Hindu friends spoke of this 'god' as one who had the courage and self-discipline to tread higher and mysterious paths. It was sometimes whispered that he had already achieved *moksha* – release from the wheel of endless rebirth. His father's life represented ultimate obedience to the Hindu scripture, the Bhagavad-Gita, which solemnly declares:

Let the Yogin ever integrate himself
Standing in a place apart,
Alone, his thoughts and self restrained,
Devoid of (earthly) hope, nothing possessing.

Let him for himself set up
A steady seat in a clean place,
Neither too high nor yet too low,
With cloth or hides or grass bestrewn.

There let him sit and make his mind a single point;
Let him restrain the motions of his thought and senses.
And engage in spiritual exercises (yoga)
To purify the self.

Remaining still, let him keep body, head and neck
In a straight line, unmoving;
Let him fix his gaze on the tip of his own nose,
Not looking round about him.

There let him sit, his self all stilled,
His fear all gone, firm in his vow of chastity,
His mind controlled, his thoughts on Me
Integrated, yet intent on Me.

It came as a tremendous shock to Rabi to learn of his father's premature death. His uncle Vishnu, frustrated and bemused by the guru, had gone to Rabi's father and had dragged him to hospital. The doctors decided that the Yogi's hair was too long and when the nurse began to cut back his unruly hair, Rabi's father fell backwards and died.

Now that his father was dead, it was Rabi's turn to become a great Yogi. Would he follow in his father's footsteps and renounce the world, its pleasures and charms, for the sake of enlightenment?

This true and macabre story can introduce us to the puzzling and mystical world of Hinduism. Why did this man renounce the world, his wife and his young son for a life of meditation in the temple? Why did he abandon all 'normal' human activities in his search for enlightenment? To answer this question we must examine some key Hindu beliefs.

Key Beliefs of Hinduism

1. Reincarnation

Hindus believe that all human beings live not one life but a series of lives on earth. The human soul remains the same but passes through a series of different bodies. Some Hindus believe that a person's soul can 'transmigrate' into the body of a bird or an insect. Here is a verse from a Hindu scripture that elucidates this belief:

As a man casts off his worn-out clothes
And takes on other new ones in their place,
So does the embodied soul cast off his worn-out bodies
And enters others new.

This belief in reincarnation contrasts strikingly with the Jewish and Christian idea of resurrection. In Christian belief all people live one life and then they are judged by God. They will appear before God not as 'souls' but as resurrected people. To an atheist, both belief in resurrection and reincarnation appear comical. When a person dies, he or she rots.

2. Caste

In India today there is a rigid caste system. Officially the system has been outlawed by the Indian government but it continues to exercise a profound influence. The word 'caste' refers to a particular social group; these castes are traditionally rooted in different types of occupation or job. There are four main caste groups; each is further sub-divided into sub-castes. They are:

1. Brahmins – priests.
2. Kshatriyas – rulers and warriors.
3. Vaishyas – tradesmen, artisans and farmers
4. Shudras – labourers.

It is often forgotten that there is a fifth group of so-called 'untouchables' or 'outcastes'. These outcastes perform the most unpleasant tasks in Indian society – street cleaning and toilet cleaning.

In the course of time, the priestly class came to occupy a position of superiority over against all other castes. A hierarchy of importance and value developed; Brahmins at the top and outcastes at the bottom. Thus people are not of equal value but are graded according to caste. Some members of the Brahmin caste will strive to avoid 'untouchable' people because they believe that this will defile them. Untouchable people are sometimes encouraged to wear bells so that higher caste people may discern their presence.

3. Karma

Traditionally Hindus have believed that the caste system has been ordained by the gods. If a person has lived a good life he or she will be reincarnated in a higher caste. To be born as an untouchable implies that one has misbehaved in previous lives. The key term here is *Karma*. Each soul collects good and bad deeds and the accumulation of these deeds determines how a soul will be reborn. A good karma will enable a soul to enter the body of a Brahmin baby; a bad karma will condemn a soul to sojourn in the body of an untouchable baby. Suffering in this life is understood as being the result of a bad karma in a previous life.

4. Maya

To the consumerist, the world is very real – it is a stockpile of raw materials that can be transformed into consumer-durables. The Hindu does not share this conviction. In the Hindu perspective, the world we perceive is no more than a creation of our own minds. The world is a mirage or a hologram; we think it is there but we are mistaken.

In the film *Total Recall*, Arnold Schwarzenegger cleverly exploits a hologram device. His enemies are very keen to 'blow him away', and are very numerous. Arnold suddenly appears and they immediately attack. Unfortunately they are pumping 'lead' into Arnold's hologram! The real Arnold suddenly appears and they themselves are blown away. This scene in the film can help us to understand the Hindu idea of *maya*.

Maya is like a veil drawn betwen people and reality, which makes things seem different from what they are. The world may seem to be changing; the world may seem to contain many different objects but this is not really the case.

But if *maya* deceives us, then what is really real? The Hindu believes that behind this veil of appearances is a divine presence. Behind the hologram, there exists an impersonal God. This God is called Brahman. Brahman is all that exists, and anything else which seems to exist is *maya*.

5. Moksha

What is the Hindu response to *maya*? The committed Hindu wishes to escape from *maya*, *karma* and reincarnation. He or she does not wish to be endlessly reborn; this cycle of birth and rebirth is a curse.

Rabi's father was seeking release from the curse of rebirth and maya. This is why he spent eight years meditating in a temple. He wanted to escape the world of *maya* and achieve union with Brahman.

When a drop of rain is falling through the sky we can speak of *this* particular drop of rain. But when the drop of rain plunges into the sea, it ceases to exist. This individual drop is no more; it has merged with the Atlantic ocean. We could say that it has become part of the ocean.

This story of a drop and its descent into the ocean can help us to understand *moksha*. This release, this disappearance of the individual, tortured soul is *moksha*. *Moksha* can also be described as the bliss that comes from no longer being able to feel pleasure or pain; the individual soul has ceased to exist, it has merged with Brahman.

6. Yoga

Most people know about the postures and the breath control exercises of yoga. But yoga is not simply physical exercise. It is a spiritual discipline with a particular spiritual goal. Yoga is a means of releasing the soul from the body and thus reaching the bliss of moksha. The word *yoga* comes from the Sanskrit root *yuj*, which means to unite. It suggests the ideas of both discipline and of union.

In about 300 BC Patanjali, a famous teacher of yoga taught that there were eight key dimensions to the practice of yoga:

1. Yama – restraint, abstention from harming others.
2. Niyama – observance, physical and mental purity.

3. Asana – physical exercise.
4. Pranayama – breath control to gain mastery of vital energy.
5. Pratyahara – withdrawal, detachment from sensuality.
6. Dharana – concentration, fixing the mind on a single point.
7. Dhyana – meditation.
8. Samadhi – self-collectedness, being able to see the object of concentration as it really is.[3]

Yoga is more complicated that many people realise. Perhaps the most famous aspect of yoga is the chanting of a mantra. Mantras are one-word spells, such as 'om', 'hrim', 'hum', and 'klam' and are often the names of some Hindu god or goddess. A student of yoga might spend twenty-four hours repeating the name 'om'.

7. The Hindu gods

When a Westerner travels to India, he or she is often surprised by the great number of Hindu gods and goddesses. Agni is the god of fire and sacrifice. Vishnu is the god of human fate and preservation. Shiva is the source of both good and evil; he is the destroyer of life and also the one who re-creates new life. Kali is the consort of Shiva; she is the great mother and the goddess of judgement and death. These are some of the most important deities.

There are also minor gods and goddesses. There is Sitola, the goddess of chickenpox and Shri Karniji, the goddess of rats. The cobra snake is also worshipped by some Hindus. There are quite literally thousands and thousands of different gods and goddesses.

For many Hindus these gods are accepted at face value. Each god exists and exercises power and authority in its particular sphere; the gods must be appeased by appropriate ritual. The Hindu refers to this appropraite ritual as *puja*. This can involve the offering of flowers, fruit, cloth, water and money.

There are other Hindus who insist that only Brahman really exists. This god is everywhere and in all things, all animals and all people (this is called pantheism). The gods and goddesses do not actually exist; they also are part of *maya*.

Buddhism

Around the year 500 BC a man called Siddartha Gautama was born. He was a prince from the Sakya tribe who lived in the foothills of the famous Himalayan mountains. For the first thirty years of his life Gautama took no interest in religious issues. As he pondered and examined life, he became acutely aware of the all-consuming nature of death, misery and suffering. This probing of life and its purpose activated a deep desire in Gautama to find enlightenment. He abandoned his princess and their children and set out as a poor traveller to find the meaning of life.

Gautama visited many famous Hindu gurus but their teachings did not satisfy him. In one famous incident, the future founder of Buddhism sat down under a Bo tree and it was here that he found enlightenment. While sitting under the tree he was overwhelmed with a yearning for *nirvana* and a desire to escape from the illusion of *maya*.

The teachings of Siddartha Gautama have become known as Buddhism and have inspired the lives of millions of people. Buddhist teachings share many similarities with Hindu teachings; indeed Buddhism may be referred to as a 'reformed' Hinduism. The major difference between the two religions resides in the fact that Buddhism rejects the Hindu pantheon of gods and goddesses. Buddhism has been described as an atheist religion and discourages belief in both God and the gods. It should also be mentioned that many Buddhists reject the caste system.

In Buddhism it is desire and attachment to material comforts that condemn a person to the curse of reincarnation. Just as the Hindu longs to escape from the wheel of rebirth, so too does the Buddhist. Buddhist philosophy emphasises the illusory nature of individual, discrete entities. The individual dog, cat, mountain or soul do not really exist! *Maya* deceives us into believing in a plurality of different entities.

The committed Buddhist believes that the way to achieve salvation is to extinguish all desire. This embraces both seemingly good desires and bad desires; the urge to play football and the craving to take drugs; all this must end. The suppression of desire will lead to the cleansing of karmic bondage and this in turn will lead to *nirvana* (freedom from rebirth). The Buddhist understanding of *nirvana* is very similar to the Hindu concept of *moksha*. The Buddhist, however, would not speak of merging with Brahman: rather he would speak of 'nothingness' or the dissolution or cessation of individual personality.

There are many different schools and sects within Buddhism but the belief in both maya and nirvana is common to all forms of Buddhism.[4]

Notes

1. Rabindranath R. Maharaj, *Death of a Guru* (Hodder and Stoughton: London, 1978), p14.
2. *Ibid.*
3. David Burnett, *Clash of Worlds* (Monarch Publications: Eastbourne, 1990), p80.
4. I am very grateful to David Burnett and his excellent book *Clash of Worlds* for many of the ideas in this chapter.

The Yogi

Read the story about the Yogi contained in the chapter on Hinduism.

For further thought

1. Why did Rabi's dad never speak to his son?
2. What is yoga?
3. Imagine that you are Rabi's uncle. Why are you so angry with Rabi's dad?

Brief Notes

To understand the life of this yogi we will need to understand the key Hindu idea of *moksha*. Rabi's father wanted to escape from the curse of reincarnation. He wanted to become one with Brahman.

Gandhi

Born on the 2nd October 1869, Mohandas Karamchand Gandhi grew up a shy but happy child. At the age of 13 he was married to a young girl called Kasturbai. This early marital union was not an unusual notion to Ghandi as he believed that one's life partner would also have been one's life partner in previous reincarnations.

As an adolescent, Mohandas enjoyed the stories of Hindu heroes and was particularly moved by the story of King Harischandra who gave up his wife and possessions and suffered privation for the sake of truth.

Shortly before he turned nineteen, Mohandas departed for England and successfully trained as a lawyer. Unfortunately, after his return to India as a barrister, his confidence was shattered by an abysmal courtroom debut and he gratefully accepted an offer of work in South Africa. However Mohandas soon discovered that Indians in South Africa were not welcomed with open arms.

Arriving in Durban, he spent a week there before travelling first-class on a train to Pretoria. During its stop at Pietermaritzburg the train took on a European passenger who immediately objected to Gandhi's presence. Railroad officials were summoned and Gandhi was asked to move to the van compartment. He refused. Then the police arrived and threw him off the train. Shocked and bewildered, he was left stranded and very angry. Gandhi resolved to challenge the treatment he had received and immediately sent a telegram of protest to the general manager.

On arriving in Pretoria he quickly established an association for Indians which was to work for justice and fairness. Their first success came when they resisted a government bill to establish a colour bar against Indians. Uniting Hindus, Parsis and Muslims, Gandhi drew up a petition of 10,000 signatures which he sent to Lord Ripon, colonial secretary in London, who subsequently refused to assent to the bill.

In the years that followed, Gandhi became a practising lawyer in South Africa. He felt that his public work would require such dedication that he must attain *brahmcharya* or total self-control, which required sexual abstention. Kasturbai submitted to this austere vow.

Gradually Gandhi developed the idea of *satyagraha*, which in rough translation means non-violent non-cooperation. It wasn't until Gandhi returned to India in 1914 that this concept of *satyagraha* captured the imagination of women and men worldwide.

Gandhi's reputation soon grew. After spending some time establishing an ashram, or spiritual community, in Ahmedabad, he was called upon to help the peasant farmers of Champaran who were suffering under a punitive rental system. Swiftly, he weighed up the situation and organised a non-violent strike. The landlords responded violently and many peasants were injured but they refused to retaliate.

The government of India, alert to the power of the peasants' resolve, established a Commission of Enquiry and invited Gandhi to participate. His suggestions were incorporated into a report and the unjust 'tinkathia' rent system was abolished and planters were obliged to return 25% of the illegally extracted rent.

Gandhi campaigned very strongly against the caste system which relegated a whole group of people to the status of 'untouchables'. He referred to these outcaste people as the Harijans. . . . the people of God. He rejected the implicit inequality of the caste system. He fasted and prayed endlessly that there should be an end to the violence between Muslim and

Hindu. In all these causes Gandhi lived out his understanding of *satyagraha*.

This pattern of non-violent resistence being met by violent reaction being in turn met by non-violent resolve, was to characterise many of the causes championed by Gandhi. Many times Gandhi would launch into a fast to the death, thereby shaming his opponents (and sometimes his fellow Indians) into changing their unjust behaviour. Undoubtedly Gandhi's radical approach has been an inspiration to many people seeking to bring about peace on earth.

For further thought

1. Why was Gandhi so concerned about the 'untouchables'?
2. What is meant by the Hindu term *brahmcharya*?
3. What is meant by the Hindu term *satyagraha*?

Source: C. Kumar and M. Puri, *Mahatma Gandhi – His Life And Influence* (Heineman, 1982).

Caste War

Surinder Singh was a young graduate with a steady job in the Indian Defence Ministry, a bureaucrat with a secure future.

Yet it was Mr Singh who arrived in the centre of Old Delhi carrying a milkcan full of petrol. There he joined university students protesting against a government decision to open 27% of government jobs to the lower castes. An upper-caste Indian, Mr Singh showered himself with petrol and set fire to himself with a cigarette lighter.

His death sparked riots in which several student protesters were shot, and opposition politicians called for the Prime Minister's resignation. Higher-caste demonstrators in Northern India torched passenger trains and public buses and battled police. Gopi Chand, a police inspector, was shot dead.

Why did Mr Singh choose such an appalling form of public suicide? Why was he so angry with a government decision to give more jobs to the poor? The answer lies in the unique social organisation of the Indian people. As a Hindu society, it was originally divided into those who belonged to classes of priests, warriors, merchants and labourers. Over the centuries the differences have become more and more acute and India is now a highly stratified society. At the very bottom of this hierarchy are the untouchables or 'outcastes' who in rural areas are banned from using public wells. These casteless people are not allowed to stand within 50 paces of a priestly Brahmin. Untouchables have a bad 'karma' and their fate is to take the very worst jobs – toilet and street cleaning.

The population of India is approximately 900 million and of these some 150 million are considered 'untouchable'. Yet many

Hindus do not believe that the caste system is unjust but defend its seeming inequalities as divine punishment and reward for deeds performed in previous lives.

Many people feel that Singh is simply one of the first casualties in a war between the castes. The upper castes in India feel threatened by the idea of lower castes gaining a competitive edge. The crisis cuts right through Indian society and many professionals believe that giving jobs to lower castes will lower the effectiveness of Indian public services.

For further thought

1. Imagine that you are an untouchable toilet cleaner. How do you feel?
2. You are a high-caste Indian and you are very angry with a new law that will help 'untouchables'. Describe how you feel.
3. Explain clearly the connection between reincarnation and the caste system.

Rat Worship

In the small village of Deshnok in North Rajastan sits the only temple in India devoted to rat worship. Every day hundreds of worshippers of the Hindu goddess Shri Karniji make the long pilgrimage to this shrine.

Shri Karniji was born in 1444 and was reputed to have lived for 151 years. It is said that she was capable of miracles. In one often recounted story, a soldier named Rama Mokal, found himself surrounded by his enemies in battle. After praying to Karniji, he received a lion in place of his horse and defeated the enemy. Karniji's modern day followers continue to seek out 'darsham' or blessing for themselves.

In her temple in Deshnok, rats are found in large numbers as they are believed to be the incarnation of the goddess. These sacred rats, or kabas, are fed on gifts of food and milk which add up to about £2,500 a year. The rats are fed around the clock so that they never leave the temple itself. At 11 o'clock every morning they cluster around a large bowl of buffalo milk set aside for them in the outer sanctum of the temple.

The journalists of India regularly voice their outrage at this practice in a country where the average wage is £400 a year and 450 million people live in poverty. Yet the devotees continue to flock in with their offerings of sweetmeats and coconuts which are presented to the head priest in exchange for a blessing and the application of kum kum, an orange dot on the forehead, the ancient symbol of the third eye.

In addition it is worth noting that an old Hindu tradition required any person who stepped on a rat and killed it to give the rat's weight in gold and silver to the temple or endure bad karma forever. This is proving a little impracticable today, and in its place the temple staff have taken to selling small silver rats to cover such an incident.

A curious modern addition to the temple are crash barriers, set up to control the thousands who stream into the inner sanctum during special worship services.

For further thought

1. Imagined that you are an Indian journalist. You are outraged by rat worship. What might you write in your newspaper?
2. Imagine that you are a committed follower of Shri Karniji. How would you defend rat worship?
3. Why are Hindus so concerned to avoid 'bad karma'?

Source: *The Correspondent* Magazine 15 July 1990

The Kumari

When Nanimaiya Sakya was four years old, she was made to sit in a circle of freshly severed buffalo heads. Despite the pool of blood that surrounded her, she did not run away or scream. Her cool reactions convinced her onlookers that she was in fact a goddess, a *kumari*. During the next eight years, she lived in a Kathmandu palace, worshipped and feared by her keepers. Even the King of Nepal would prostrate himself before her, begging permission to continue his reign.

This Nepalese tradition of choosing young girls to worship as virgin goddesses has been going on since the sixth century. The girls are usually kept in a palace in just two or three rooms and receive little or no education. After all, what can you teach a goddess? Indeed the girl is considered to be the manifestation of a particularly short-tempered goddess known as Taleju, famous for demon-slaying.

Once on her throne the goddess gives an audience to hundreds of worshippers every day. Her every action and reaction is weighed with the utmost gravity. Three days after one *kumari* had chipped a tooth, a large earthquake shook Nepal. Another time when a king (Tribhuvan) was taken for his anointing, the *kumari* kept trying to anoint the prince. Soon after, the king died and the prince took the throne.

The goddess, however, is only deemed worthy of worship while she is 'pure'. As soon as menstruation begins, another candidate is sought. The fall from grace for these girls can be devastating. Men are afraid of them and they often end up as prostitutes or vagrants, wandering the streets alone and abandoned. Not surprisingly the goddesses are not allowed to keep any of the many gifts that are given to them during their reign.

For further thought

1. Who are the *kumari* and why are they worshipped?
2. Can you think of any other human-beings who are wor-shipped as gods?
3. You are a *kumari* and you have just had your first period. How do you feel?

Brief Notes

The ancient Roman emperors were sometimes worshipped as gods. Even until quite recently, the Japanese emperors were believed to be divine. There are even those who consider Elvis Presley to be a god!

Source: 'The Goddesses', *The Independent*, 21 March 1992.

Marathon Monks

In 1986, Tanno, a Buddhist monk, committed himself on pain of death to complete the 1000 marathons of Mount Heie. He had seven years in which to cover over 27,000 miles. If he could complete the tasks set him, he would become a living Buddha and only the sixth man since 1945 to achieve this exalted status through the marathons.

In the first three years he completed 300 marathons; this phase of the marathon has become known as the stage of 'walking hell'. He suffered agonising back pain, endless torn muscles, high fevers and frequent bouts of diarrhoea. Nevertheless he perfected the technique of walking without moving any part of his upper body.

In the next two years he walked an incredible 400 marathons. Having agreed to take on this challenge, Tanno cannot utter a word of complaint as this would show a loss of heart. Indeed if he failed to complete the test he would have to commit suicide.

The tradition of the marathons dates back 1100 years and is born out of the Buddhist belief that the root of all suffering is the self or ego. Only by meditation and austerity can people come to see the illusory nature of self and so move beyond this to discover the divine nature – the Buddha within.

Many Buddhists believe that enlightenment (removal of the self from the cycle of reincarnation) can only be achieved after many reincarnations. Not so the marathon monks of Mount Heie in Japan. They believe that the practice of extreme austerity needed to complete the marathon program will mean that the process can be completed in one lifetime.

Tanno is also required to renounce all personal possessions

and to renounce his family, whom he must see as little as possible. In addition, once the first 700 marathons are completed, he must face the Great Fast. Nine days without any food or drink. According to Western medical experts, a normal human body would die in about seven days under the conditions Tanno must endure. During the fast Tanno continuously recited 100,000 mantras. Amazingly he survived the ordeal, having lost one quarter of his bodyweight.

In the final year Tanno had to complete one hundred 52 mile marathons on consecutive days, with only two hours of sleep per day.

Even as his devotees were hailing him as a living Buddha, his master was quietly explaining to him that:

'the real journey begins now.'

For further thought

1. Why must Tanno renounce his family and all his possessions?
2. What are mantras?
3. What does Tanno hope to achieve by undergoing his incredible marathon?

Source: *The Marathon Monks of Mount Heie* Channel 4 May 25th 1993.

COMMUNISM

INTRODUCTION

Kim Philby was one of the most remarkable spies ever to have lived. He was born in India on the 1st of January 1912. Kim came from an upper-class family and he went to the famous Westminster public school.

In 1929 Kim went up to Trinity College, Cambridge to read history. The Cambridge which welcomed Kim was a bastion of ruling-class privilege. It was a Cambridge of parties, idle frolicing, punts and strawberry teas.

Philby began to meet a lot of people who were becoming increasingly disillusioned with this world of wealth and privilege. Philby started to flirt with left-wing ideas and in 1932 he became the treasurer of the Cambridge University Socialist Society.

Philby was on the verge of becoming a communist. In an interview he explained as follows:

> I had already decided at nineteen, after a good look around me, that the rich had had it too damned good for too damned long and that the poor had had it too damned bad and that it was time that it was changed. In England at that time the poor really were a different people. It wasn't just a question of some of us being better off. With many of the poor it was a question of getting something to eat. People like my grandmother thought that was the natural way of

things. I can remember her making remarks like, 'Don't play with those children, Kim. They're dirty and you'll catch something.'[1]

Philby became aware of the rise of the Nazi party in Germany and he came to believe that communism was the only answer to this threatening and aggressive movement. Philby spent a lot of time with Donald Maclean, Anthony Blunt and Guy Burgess; these men were also communist sympathisers.

In about 1934 Philby was approached by a man who asked him if he would like to join the Russian intelligence service. Kim accepted this invitation and set about his life's work – to penetrate the British Special Intelligence Service (SIS). Philby's Cambridge friends, Maclean, Blunt and Burgess were also recruited by the Russian intelligence service at about the same time.

He quickly 'shed' his communist beliefs and past and became a thoroughly respectable English gentlemen. He served as a newspaper correspondent during the Spanish Civil War and became noted for his conservative political leanings. Philby was to maintain this mask of deception for many years.

In 1940 he was recruited by the SIS and eventually he became the head of the anti-Soviet section. This effectively meant that the man who was running secret operations against the Russians was a Russian agent himself!

In such a position of power and influence, Philby was able to provide his Russian masters with dangerous information. He informed them of the activities of all British agents working in the Soviet Union; many of these men and women were killed by the KGB (Russian Secret Intelligence) as a direct consequence of Philby's commitment to the Soviet Union.

There was even a time when Philby was being groomed to become 'C', the head of SIS but this was not to be. In 1963, Philby was unmasked and he defected to Moscow where he spent the remaining years of his life. When he died in 1988, he was given a hero's funeral by his employers, the KGB.

This true and intriguing spy story can serve as an introduction to 'communism'. Philby became a spy because he had become a communist. He was not interested in the extra income! He became a spy because he had come to believe that the world's problems could be solved by a communist revolution. He had come to believe that he could best serve the spread of communism by infiltrating the SIS and betraying its secrets to his Soviet controllers. Philby's commitment to communism is expressed very clearly in a revealing dialogue with his third wife, Eleanor:

> Puzzling over Philby's interrogation of her about her contacts with the CIA and SIS, Eleanor waited her moment and then asked Philby outright: 'What is more important in your life, me and the children or the Communist Party?' He answered firmly and without a moment's hesitation: 'The Party, of course.'[2]

Philby was, without doubt, supremely committed to the communist movement but what exactly is communism? We will now briefly examine some of the key communist beliefs that prompted Philby to betray his country.

Key Beliefs of Communism

1. Religion is the Opium of the People

The most influential communist writer is, without doubt, Karl Marx. Marx was born in Trier in Germany in 1818 and he died in 1883. His ideas and convictions have had an astonishing impact upon the twentieth century.

Marx was a committed atheist. He rejected God and the gods. He believed that 'religion' was the opium of the people. Drugs can distract us from the real business of life. Marx believed that 'religion' encouraged people to be otherwordly, to dream of heaven and so to forget the misery and sadness of their poverty-striken lives. He wrote: 'The criticism of religion ends with the teaching that man is the highest being for man.'

Marx believed that only humans and nature exist; in many ways consumerism and communism share similar assumptions about the meaning of life. God and the pagan gods do not exist. Human-beings must live their lives without 'higher' beings; humans must master and conquer nature on their own.

2. Human-beings are intrinsically Good.

Marx believed that women and men are intrinsically good. This belief contrasts strikingly with the nihilist attitude to life. The communist tends to believe that human-beings do bad things because they are corrupted by greedy and unjust societies. Corrupt societies encourage selfishness, laziness and cruelty. But the individual is really cooperative, generous and potentially perfect. Change the society and the individual will change too.

3. Science and Technology are making Great Progress.

We could say that the Marxist has a very high view of humankind. He or she is, at root, very virtuous. Marx also believed that human-beings are extremely clever and rational. Science and technology are human activities that humans can exploit to increase their knowledge and mastery of nature. If man can only tame and conquer a hostile world, he will usher in a perfect world. The human ability to devise clever machines and tools is very significant. In the 1920's Russian communists would sing the following song:

> Electricity can do anything. It can dispel darkness and gloom.
> One push of a button and clickety-click out comes a new man.[3]

This Russian song betrays a key Marxist hope. Science has the power not only to create enormous wealth but further to transform man himself. Trotsky, a famous communist, once declared, 'Such is the power of science, that the average human-being will become an Aristotle, a Goethe, a Marx. And beyond this, new peaks will rise.'[4]

This faith in science is filled with optimism and hope. Progress in science and technology will provide abundant food, clothing and numerous consumer-durables. Poverty and destitution will vanish. Science will also transform human beings into gods!

4. Only a Minority benefit from the Fruits of Progress

But, says the Marxist, only the rich and privileged are benefitting from this astonishing progress. Only the factory owners and the land owners are enjoying nature's bounty. The rest of the world's population are being exploited. Aristocrats and successful business tycoons quaff champagne and nibble on expensive caviar while the 'workers' are labouring night and day for a pittance.

In his famous work *Das Kapital*, Marx described how a seven-year-old boy, William Wood, had to bring ready-moulded articles to a drying room, day in and day out, from six o'clock in the morning until nine at night. Marx was understandably appalled by this tragedy. And yet this kind of exploitation was all too common in nineteenth century England.

5. Capitalism exploits most People

Marx was angry with a society where only a privileged minority owned all the land and factories. He called this type of society – capitalist. Marx argued that in a capitalist society, working people do not enjoy the fruit of their labour. They work very hard all day long and then receive very little reward. At the same time rich people can loaf around, sipping expensive wine, feasting on the finest fillet steak and indulging in the pleasures of canasta. All this leisure and pleasure is only possible because the workers are forced to beaver away unstintingly. Marx believed that the rich were feasting and supping at the expense of the working classes. The rich dined and the poor man was forced to foot the bill.

6. Class struggle

Marx argued that capitalism, although morally repugnant, was a necessary stage on the road to a communist society. Capitalism, although a superb provider, is a poor and unjust distributor of the fruits of progress. A capitalist society is able to generate huge wealth but it rewards only a tiny minority.

Marx believed that progress does not develop smoothly and effortlessly. Progress can only come about by conflict. In particular he believed that the history of the world is the history of class struggle.

In the ancient world rulers owned slaves and this scenario brought conflict between the ruler and the slaves he exploited. The famous film *Spartacus* depicts this conflict very convincingly. This phase in human history was replaced by feudalism. In this type of society, the serf was no longer a slave but was allowed to work his lord's land on the condition of handing over a percentage of his harvest to his lord and master. Feudalism had given way to capitalism with the coming of the Industrial Revolution. Lords and serfs had been replaced by owners and workers. Marx argued that capitalism, in its turn, would give way to a communist society.

History is the history of class struggle; each society was morally superior to the last. With the disappearance of class conflict, a perfect communist society would then hold sway.

7. A Revolution is Required

How then would this new communist world come into being?

Marx did not believe that the owners of land, money and factories would voluntarily hand over their great wealth to the working classes. Such people benefitted greatly from their exploitation of the working people. Marx believed that only a violent revolution could usher in this new communist world. In his famous work *The Communist Manifesto*, Marx is most emphatic about this:

> The Communists disdain to conceal their views and aims. They openly declare that their ends can be obtained only by the forcible overthrow of all existing social conditions. Let the ruling class tremble at a Communistic revolution. The proletarians have nothing to

lose but their chains. They have a world to win.
WORKING MEN OF ALL COUNTRIES, UNITE![5]

8. After the Revolution the State will Wither away

The Communist revolution would abolish all private property. Individual people would no longer own land or factories. All wealth would belong to the 'workers'. Marx believed that the state would eventually wither away because the power of science and progress would transform all people into cooperative and virtuous citizens. The need for armies, policing and 'law and order' would no longer exist. A new communist citizen would emerge, sociable, cooperative and happy. An enormously productive economy would provide sufficient wealth for all people.

In 1961 the Communist Party Programme of the Soviet Union described communism as follows:

> Communism is a classless social system with one single form of public ownership of the means of production and full social equality of all members of society; under it, the all-round development of people will be accompanied by the growth of the productive forces through continuous progress in science and technology; all the springs of collective wealth will flow more abundantly, and the great principle 'From each according to his ability to each according to his needs' will be implemented.[6]

Conclusion

Karl Marx, himself, was not to witness the revolution he longed to see. In 1917 there was a communist revolution in Russia; Lenin, a disciple of Karl Marx, became the first leader of a communist society. Lenin developed Marx's ideas and faced the practical difficulties of organising a communist society. He made some startling declarations:

> The Communist must be prepared to make every sacrifice, and, if necessary, even to resort to all sorts of cunning, schemes and stratagems, to employ illegal methods, to evade and conceal the truth.[7]

Lenin taught a doctrine of sacrifice, or sacrificial readiness, saying that the revolution is a time to wade through streams of blood. Perhaps Kim Philby had read this. Perhaps this most remarkable spy had fully understood Lenin's doctrine of sacrifice. Indeed he was willing to sacrifice everything for the sake of revolution. . . . . . . his marriage to his wife Eleanor and even the lives of fellow colleagues in the SIS!

Notes

1. Phillip Knightly, *Philby: The Life and Views of a Masterspy* (Andre Deutsch Ltd: London, 1988), p33.
2. *Ibid*, p229.
3. Taken from *Pandora's Box* BBC 2, 29th July 1993.
4. *Ibid*.
5. Karl Marx and Friedrich Engels, *The Communist Manifesto* (Oxford University Press; Oxford, 1992), p39.
6. Quoted by Nikita Khrushchev in 'On the Communist Party,' Krushchev's report on the Communist Party Program to the 22nd Congress of the Party (Foreign Languages Publishing House: Moscow, 1961), p27.
7. As quoted by Bob Goudzwaard, *Idols of our Time* (Inter-Varsity Press: Illinois, 1984), p32.

Kim Philby, the Spy

This story can be found at the beginning of this chapter.

For further thought

1. Give three different reasons why a person might become a spy.
2. Why did Kim Philby become a spy?
3. What impact did Philby's commitment to communism have upon his personal life?

Brief Notes

For some people the motivation to become a spy might involve patriotism. For others there might be a fascination with the seeming glamour of espionage. Philby became a spy because of his commitment to communism and the Soviet Union.

Che Guevara

The life of Che Guevara, one of the leading revolutionaries of this century, was neatly summarized by a statement he himself made:

> I was born in Argentina, I fought in Cuba, and I began to be a revolutionary in Guatemala.

However, contrary to expectation, Che, or to give him his full title, Ernesto Guevara de la Serna, was actually born into a privileged Spanish/Irish family in Argentina in 1928.

Crucially, his parents encouraged him to be free-thinking and critically aware. As a family friend, Ricardo Rojo noted that in the Guevara household there existed: 'a passion for justice, the rejection of fascism, religious indifference, an interest in literature and love of poetry, and a prejudice against money and the ways of making it.'

As a youth, Che was dynamic, unconventional and independent in outlook. He constantly defied any problems that set him back, particularly a severe asthma complaint. This drove him to become a prominent athlete and itinerant traveller and enabled him to complete a six year University course in just three years, passing sixteen major exams in six months despite forty-five severe asthma attacks. Ironically, at eighteen years of age, he was rejected for military service.

Che decided to take up medical studies, albeit in a somewhat sporadic fashion. His desire for 'hitting the road' was deep-set and on one occasion he and a friend Alberto Granados took off on a hobos tour of Latin America.

Taking up menial jobs to pay his way, Che was able to observe at first hand the living conditions of the bulk of the Latin American population. He saw a dispossessed and poverty stricken people, crushed by a privileged elite. This experience was to affect Che deeply.

By 1953 Che had completed his studies and visited Bolivia to support the new reformed government. However, his attempts to relate to the Bolivian Indians proved frustrating and he and his friends moved on to Guatemala. Here Che was to meet up with Jacobo Arbenz, head of the Guatemalen government. Arbenz argued passionately that: 'Man is not just a stomach. We believe that, above all, he hungers for dignity.'

Boldly, Arbenz nationalized the United Fruit Company, in defiance of the United States. The reaction to this was swift and devastating. The CIA began training the troops of rebel Castillo Armas and supplied them with weapons and ammunition. A brief and bloody coup d'etat ensued and the Arbenz regime was toppled.

Che was suddenly vulnerable and retreated to the safety of the Argentine embassy. Eventually he was able to escape to Mexico City where he began to study revolutionary theory in much greater depth. His passion for justice grew and was to find its focus after a meeting with Fidel Castro.

Having failed once to overthrow the Cuban regime, Castro was keen to assemble a new army and signed up Che and a motley assortment of amateur revolutionaries. A total of eighty two men set out to remove the dictator Fulgencio Batisto.

Sadly their skill did not match their enthusiasm. A tragic succession of basic military errors led to their betrayal and ambush, reducing their number to just twelve.

Fortunately the local peasants supported them in their desperate plight and slowly they were able to renew their strength. In 1957 they made their first successful attack on the La Plata barracks. With their morale boosted they launched more raids and became a shrewd, battle-hardened force. New recruits were still hard to come by, but the local peasants supported them with food, shelter and information.

Their fame grew, greatly aided by their insistence on humane treatment of their enemy; Che developed new organisational skills to facilitate the continued efforts of the guerilla force.

In 1959 the Cuban government was overthrown and the guerillas faced a new challenge; running the country. Che took on the task of putting together a coherent and systematic ideological stance. Perhaps surprisingly, it was only at this point that Che embraced communism. Che, however, remained sceptical of the official Soviet outlook. In his book *Guerilla Warfare* he argued that a rural uprising was the best route to revolutionary success. In the six years that Che remained in Cuba, he took up a variety of ministerial posts in an attempt to press home long cherished agrarian reforms.

At heart though, Che was a fighter and he became bored with the intricacies and challenges of government. In 1965 he and a handful of veterans left for Bolivia to aid the revolutionary movement in the very centre of Latin America. Bolivia, however, proved a much tougher proposition than Cuba. The guerillas were never able to mobilize popular peasant support and were constantly betrayed and isolated. Che was eventually captured and executed with much pomp and ceremony. His body was burnt and his ashes spread over the continent for which he had given his life.

For further thought

1. In what sense can we refer to Che Guevara as a Marxist?
2. How did Che Guevara criticise orthodox Marxism?
3. Why do you think that Che Guevara became a revolutionary?

Source: Frank Kermode, *Guevara* (Fontana, 1970).

The life of Josef Stalin

At the height of his reign, Alexei Tolstoy declared of Stalin:–

Thou bright sun of the nations.
The unsinking sun of our times.
And more than the sun, for the sun has no wisdom.

Yet in just thirty years of power Josef Stalin had killed more people than the merciless Tsars had managed to eliminate in 400
years. Lenin himself was uneasy about the rise of young Josef in
the Party: 'Comrade Stalin has concentrated boundless authority
in his hands and I am not sure whether he will always be capable
of using that authority with sufficient caution. . .'

But Stalin was a skilful political operator and was able to
demote, expel and exile all his key rivals. More than anything,
Stalin wanted to make the Soviet Union a world power through
rapid industrialisation. Coal, iron and steel production were
paramount and loss of human life in the process was seen as
insignificant. Richer peasants were taxed heavily; their land was
taken and they were ordered to join vast collective farms. The
less fortunate were herded into cities to work in the factories and
those who resisted were transported to the infamous labour
camps. All in all more than 25 million people were driven off
their land and over 3 million were killed. Stalin summed up his
approach most succinctly: 'The death of a man is a tragedy; the
death of a thousand is a statistic.'

His wife Nadezhda Alliluevna eventually committed suicide
in 1932, so appalled was she by his brutality. He regularly
abused those around him in fits of drunken rage but was also

careful to remove potential enemies. By 1939, 98 of the 139-strong Central Committee had been shot! Any hint of conspiracy was dealt with mercilessly and anyone having knowledge of his misdeeds was as good as dead.

Stalin was a pragmatic leader, willing to make any deal to advance his purposes. With the advent of World War II, he signed a pact with Hitler that gave him even more opportunity to inflict terror on innocent people. In the Ukrainian town of Vinnitsa (population 70,000) a mass grave of 9,000 people was uncovered; the bodies had been carefully laid head to toe to save space.

Perhaps not surprisingly, Stalin lived in constant fear for his life. He always wore a bullet proof vest and only made public appearances in an armoured car with three inch thick bullet proof glass. But death was to catch up with him finally in the form of a cerebral haemorrhage in 1953.

In a nation of 200 million people, he had a truly devastating impact. In the words of Alexei Tolstoy, 'scarcely a family had been untouched by tragedy'.

For further thought

1. Why was Stalin so keen to industralise the Soviet Union?
2. 'The death of a man is a tragedy; the death of a thousand is a statistic.' Discuss.
3. You are a journalist and a member of the Communist Party. The editor of your newspaper has asked you to write an article in support of communism. What would you write?

Brief Notes

For Marx, capitalism is a necessary stage on the road to the communist society. Capitalism and its industrial capacity are superb providers of wealth. Communism, like capitalism, embraces a profound faith in science and technology. Rapid industrialisation is key to both ideologies.

Alexander Solzhenitsyn

In 1945 in East Prussia a young and courageous Russian soldier had begun to criticise Stalin's 'cult of personality' in his correspondence with friends. Unfortunately Alexander Solzhenitsyn's honesty was soon to place him in great peril. An organisation known as 'Smersh' (an acronym for 'death to spies') was alerted to his anti-Stalinist tendences.

Alexander was then summoned to the local military headquarters by his commanding officer. Solzhenitsyn expected a routine discussion of his recent military conduct but was surprised when he was ordered to surrender his revolver. Presently his captain's insignia were ripped off by Smersh agents; Solzhenitsyn resisted the assault. However his commanding officer dropped a hint about the nature of his arrest and Solzhenitsyn submitted.

Solzhenitsyn, now a 'dirty counter' (a counter-revolutionary) was transported to Moscow. His destination was Lubyanka, the headquarters of the Soviet Security apparatus. Ironically, upon arrival in Moscow, his escort had no idea where the building was and Solzhenitsyn found himself directing him to the building from which barely one in ten thousand prisoners ever walked free.

Not surprisingly, young Alexander, like the other inmates of Lubyanka, was quickly subjected to a humiliating strip search. This was then followed by brutal deprivation and harsh interrogation. The aim was quite simply to extract a confession regardless of evidence (as was the case with countless other detainees). After all, according to Andrey Vyshinsky, Stalin's chief legal theoretician, 'Confession is the queen of evidence.'

Solzhenitsyn experienced the full horror of a device known as a box. These 'boxes' were 'dazzlingly whitewashed and blindingly lit' and were so small that one could not even sit down properly in them. He was forced to remain in such 'boxes' for long periods of time.

Solzhenitsyn's crime was one of thought: entertaining and imparting prohibited ideas. Seemingly this merited all manner of torture by his captors. Yet he confessed to nothing and could not be convinced to name other 'guilty' persons.

When his case was finally heard on July 7th, 1945, his prospects were poor. He had dared to criticise Stalin's credentials as a Marxist-Leninist, while upholding the correctness of the theory. In the light of this daring criticism, his eight year sentence in a 'corrective-labour' camp was fairly lenient and reflected the inconsistency of Soviet justice.

Solzhenitsyn soon discovered that life in these camps was a 'teeth-grinding struggle for survival'. Indeed, so harsh was the life that, were it not for a stroke of luck, he would almost certainly have died. Fortuitously, after it became known that he was a scientist, he was removed from the labour-camp and put to work in a research establishment within a prison.

Years later, after his release, he developed and recovered from cancer, as well as suffering the pain of exile. Despite all this he went on to become one of Russia's greatest living authors and to expose with his brilliant works of literature the brutality of a regime dedicated to its own survival.

For further thought

1. You are Stalin. What would you say to Alexander Solzhenitsyn?
2. Discuss the statement, 'Confession is the queen of evidence.'
3. You are an inmate of a Soviet labour camp. You have bribed a guard to smuggle a letter to your family. What would you write?

Source: D. Burg and G. Feifer, *Solzhenitsyn – A Biography* (Hodder & Stoughton: London, 1972).

Pol Pot

Pol Pot, whose name is inextricably linked with Cambodia's 'killing fields' in world history, grew up as a peasant under the authoritarian reign of Prince Sihanouk. Whilst relatively peaceful and prosperous compared with Cambodia's neighbouring nations, it was a time of great instability including many human rights violations and savagery between warring groups. After a period of time as a Buddhist monk, Pol Pot travelled to Paris during the 1950's to study electronics on a scholarship.

During his time in Paris, Pol Pot and fellow Cambodian Khieu Samphan became attracted to the left wing ideas current at that time. The challenge for them was to eliminate the vestiges of colonial rule and avoid captialist exploitation at the same time. Thus, Khieu Samphan developed his philosophy of rural revolution. He believed that the solution to getting rid of colonialism and preventing the rise of capitalism was for Cambodia to become a peasant economy – bereft of towns, currency, industry or education.

Upon their return to Cambodia, both Pol Pot and Khieu Samphan joined the Chinese-backed communist party, later known as the Khmer Rouge and worked for the overthrow of President Lon Nol's government which had been in power since 1970. By 1975 they had achieved their aim and were in positions of sufficient power to put their radical theories into practice. With Khieu Samphan as a titular leader and Pol Pot effectively holding the power, they wanted nothing less than complete revolution.

Their revolution was initiated on April 17, 1975, known as the first day of 'Year Zero', by a mass eviction of the more than two million residents of the capital city of Phenom Penh. They were told to leave under the pretence that Pol Pot wanted the city temporarily evacuated to make it safe against American bombing. Aside from a few thousand who were to maintain the city, everyone, regardless of what condition they were in, was forced to march to the countryside and join vast rural communes. No one was allowed to take any possessions and anyone not able to sustain the journey was either left alone to starve or clubbed to death. This process continued until every town and village had been emptied and every citizen had been assigned a task in the fields.

Each person was forced to work eleven hours a day for nine days at a time. On the tenth day they enjoyed the privilege of political education. Surrounded by malaria-ridden swamps and fed on gruel and fish with no medical care, death soon claimed many members of the Cambodian population. Those that were able to survive these conditions had to get used to living a very barren existence. No possessions aside from a sleeping mat and a pair of black overalls were permitted. Most material possessions of the pre Pol Pot era including cars, machines and appliances had been simply left to rot and rust. No longer was there any property, trade, industry, money or market place.

As all schools were abolished, children were forced to begin work at the age of seven. In fact all books had been burnt and the National Library converted into a pigsty. Anyone who was considered to be a member of the educated classes was executed as was anyone who dared to utter a word of complaint. As a warning to those who would consider resistence to the regime, the latter were frequently buried to the neck and left to die.

This experiment in human community lasted four years until the Vietnamese army invaded the country. Pol Pot's army was defeated but he escaped to the hills in Thailand and remains there now near the Cambodian border as the head of the Khmer People's National Liberation Front. The devastation discovered by the Vietnamese in 1979 horrified them beyond belief.

Not long after Pol Pot's removal from office, his foreign minister Ieng Sary admitted to three million deaths in just four years. In a country of eight million people, nearly half the population had been decimated. Sary asserted that the orders from Pol Pot has been 'misunderstood'. The massacres were simply a 'mistake'.

For further thought

1. You have just been 'liberated' of all your possessions and you have been frog-marched into the countryside to work on the land. You are an educated person. How might you feel?
2. Why might totalitarian regimes have a problem with educated citizens?
3. How would an orthodox Marxist criticise the vision and practice of Pol Pot?

Source: *Crooks, Crime and Corruption*, No single author (Chancellor Press: London, 1987).
John Pilger, *Heroes* (Pan Books: London, 1986).

Robert Owen

Robert Owen was a man motivated by the notion that utopia, a perfect human community, was possible. After making his fortune in the cotton industry in Manchester he decided to move north to Lanark, in 1799, and form a partnership with David Dale, lay preacher, philanthropist and industrialist.

Owen wasted no time in introducing a host of new working practices in the cotton mill. This included a reduction in working hours, the introduction of sick pay and pension schemes. He also opened a shop which sold good quality products at a low price. Swiftly he won the confidence of the workforce and the factory prospered. This served to confirm in Owen's mind the dictum that 'the character of man is made for him and not by him'. He believed that by changing a person's environment, it was possible to change the person's character. Indeed it was Owen's aim to create an environment that would produce happiness, for he believed that happiness 'will be the only religion of man'.

In 1815, after the Napoleonic War, there was a sharp slump in the British economy which brought widespread poverty and unemployment. Owen proposed the establishment of self-sufficient agricultural communities, declaring that they could transform society and inaugurate the 'New Moral World'. Unfortunately, Owen was too radical and critical, and after a barbed attack on established religion, he was forced to abandon any possibility of government support for his utopian projects.

Confident that his scheme could work, Owen seized an opportunity presented to him by Richard Flower. A community in Indiana, USA, called Harmony was up for sale and Owen bought it lock, stock and barrel for a knock-down price of

$150,000. Thus, in 1824, New Harmony was born, America's first secular utopian experiment.

In its early days, Owen entrusted the community with a three-year transitional plan to put into practice and a school was set up but very little was actually produced. Disappointed, Owen returned to the community after one year and cut short the plan by introducing the 'New Harmony Community of Equals'. This, however, was to precipitate the first split and a William Maclure took his followers and set up Macluria, an alternative 'utopia', on the same estate. The two groups remained friendly but in 1826 disputes about ownership and authority became so ferocious that a third group was formed called Feiba Peven.

Undeterred, Owen was still able to proclaim on July 4th 1826 that his community had been liberated from the 'monstrous evils' of 'Private or Individual Property, Absurd or Irrational systems of Religion and Marriage founded on Individual Property'. Furthermore he declared that New Harmony was the beginning of the millenium.

Disputes continued apace at New Harmony and gradually the experiment began to disintegrate. Owen was sustaining heavy financial losses and he tried to retrieve some of this by selling a portion of the estate. This was not a popular move and Owen decided to abandon his utopian dreams in June 1827 and bequeathed the land to his children and his friend William Maclure.

Owen's attempt to create a perfect society failed dismally; it had the effect, however, of inspiring many more 'utopian experiments'.

For further thought

1. What is meant by the term 'utopia'?
2. Why do many communists want to abolish 'private property'?
3. Is communism an optimistic or a pessimistic belief-system? Give reasons for your answer.

ORPHISM AND GNOSTICISM

INTRODUCTION

Simeon Stylites was born in the year 409 AD and grew up as a shepherd boy. However his real longing was to enter a monastic order and to endure the austerities that he hoped would bring him closer to God.

Unfortunately for Simeon his enthusiasm for austerity soon got him into trouble. Having gained entry to a monastery, he so shocked his brother monks with his extreme self-denial, that they asked him to leave.

Unperturbed, Simeon became a hermit and began a new and rather unusual way of life. He built a column six feet high in the Syrian desert and lived on it for several years! Simeon, however, was rather ashamed of this small pillar. After a determined search he found a sixty foot pillar situated thirty miles from Antioch in a sun-scorched wilderness. This pillar was perfect; it was three feet across with a railing to prevent him from falling off in his sleep. Will Durant continues the story:

> On this perch Simeon lived uninterruptedly for thirty years, exposed to rain and sun and cold. A ladder enabled disciples to take him food and remove his waste. He bound himself to the pillar by a rope; the rope became embedded in his flesh, which putrified around it, and stank, and teemed with worms. Simeon picked up the worms that fell from his sores, and replaced them there, saying to them, 'Eat what God has given you.'[1]

133

Simeon lived on this pillar for thirty-seven years in every extreme of weather, praying and posturing or standing with arms outstretched in the form of a cross for as long as eight hours at a time.

At times he would bow down repeatedly, his head almost touching his feet. He was once seen to repeat this gesture 1,240 times before collapsing on his pillar. Many people came to worship him. Amazingly Simeon inspired many other 'stylites' (from the Greek 'stylos' or pillar) and they could be found even up until the nineteenth century in Russia.

This amazing story can introduce us to a very unusual way of life. The 'stylites' lived on pillars and sometimes for many years. Why did they do this? Why did they give everything up to live on pillars? To understand this we will need to explore the bizarre world of Orphism and gnosticism.

1. The Orphic Movement

The Orphic movement appeared in Greece in the sixth century BC. The evidence we have suggests that the followers of this movement were very interested in purification-rituals and living an austere and ascetic life. To be ascetic means to live a solitary and self-denying kind of life; pleasure, frivolity and fun are not encouraged.

The Orphics were inspired by the following 'creation' myth. Dionysius Zagreus was the son of the great god Zeus. In a terrifying battle with the mighty Titans, the evil enemies of the gods, Dionysius turned himself into a bull. The Titans pounced on him, tore him apart and devoured him. When Zeus realised that his son had been killed by the wicked Titans, he is said to have hurled a thunderbolt which burned up the Titans. Out of the ashes rose the human race. The Orphics concluded from this that human beings are composed of a divine spark (the part from Dionysius) and a body (the evil part from the Titans).

The Orphic followers worshipped Dionysius Zagreus and they came to believe that a part of the god was trapped inside their own bodies! In some sense the god was imprisoned inside all human beings. A. H. Armstrong explains as follows:

> Thus man is a blend of divine and earthly nature, and the purification and release of the divine element is the end to which the Orphic way of life is directed. The soul, it seems, to the Orphics (and this is a new idea in the Greek world) was an immortal god imprisoned in the body and doomed, unless released by following the Orphic way of life, to go around the wheel of reincarnation in an endless succession of lives, animal and human . . . By ritual purifications, by an ascetic life of which the most important feature was abstinence from animal flesh, and by knowledge of the correct magic formulae to use on the journey after death, the Orphics hoped to win release from the body and return it to the company of the gods.[2]

These Orphic ideas have had a profound influence upon the ancient Greek philosophers Pythagoras and Plato. They have also influenced 'gnostic' teachers such as Marcion and Valentinus. We will briefly examine three groups of people who have been inspired by Orphic ideas.

2. The Gnostics

Gnosticism, as we know it today, became influential in the second century AD. Some gnostics were avowedly anti-Christian but some believed that their teachings were compatible with Christian beliefs. A leading 'church father' Irenaeus, the Bishop of Lyons, believed that gnostic leanings were extremely dangerous.

There were many different gnostic sects and gnosticism cannot be reduced to a single creed (statement of belief). But it is possible to summarise basic gnostic attitudes. The world is perceived as intrinsically evil, having been created by an inferior and ignorant 'demi-urge'. This minor or inferior god actually made a mistake when he created the earth! The highest God had created heaven and this was a good place where rational spirits could contemplate without the cloying presence of 'matter'.

Unfortunately these divine spirits rebelled against the good God and as a punishment were forced to leave heaven and enter the demi-urge's creation (earth) as an appropriate punishment. Accordingly some human beings (not all) have a spark of the divine trapped or imprisoned inside their bodies. These sparks of the divine are extremely unhappy; they are exiles in a world that they detest.

But salvation is available to those with the divine spark, and comes in the form of a messenger from the 'high' god who reminds them that they are indeed lonely exiles! This 'reminding' takes the form of secret teachings and secret knowledge (gnosis) which has the power to release the imprisoned exile from the poison of the material world. Once released the gnostic begins a journey that will take it back home – ie heaven. The passage from exile back to heaven was through the knowledge of the correct password.

Some gnostic sects forbade marriage, sexual activity and the eating of meat. The gnostic devotee was encouraged to live an ascetic, self-denying way of life. Some gnostic sects were even more extreme than this and actively encouraged its devotees to 'punish' their bodies. Simeon is an example of this type of gnostic attitude. As can be clearly seen, this attitude to life is very similar to Orphism.

3. Origen

There were even those who cut off parts of their bodies in their desire to reject all attachment to the body and the world. It is believed by some scholars that the second century church father, Origen, castrated himself in this endeavour. We will briefly examine Origen's theological system.

The first creation according to Origen was that of a community of rational disembodied spirits, all equal and possessed of free will. The spirits of this community sinned and fell in varying degrees and according to their degree of sin they became angels, men or even demons.

Origen believed that the material world was only created after this primal fall as a place of punishment. The material world has been created by God as a response to sin! Its purpose is to serve as a purgatory and it would have been much better if it had never existed. Origen's position differed from the gnostics in that the material world had not been created by an ignorant demi-urge, it had been created by God.

Origen followed the Orphic tradition in believing in reincarnation. The fallen spirits were forced in their exile to pass through long series of lives moving up and down the hierarchy; sometimes a woman, sometimes an angel, sometimes even a devil. Each entombed spirit must work through its karma before it can return home to the ethereal, heavenly realm. Finally, Origen believed, all spirits would return home to their first purity and equality. Even the devils would be restored to their heavenly bliss.

Such, in brief, was Origen's theology and it bears a striking resemblance to Orphism and gnosticism, although it is adapted to a Christian context.

4. *The Jains*

It is even possible to find twentieth-century people who embrace very similar beliefs to the Orphics and the Gnostics. The Jains are an outstanding example. Jainism is a religion of intense austerities. It would be inaccurate to say that Jainism has developed from Orphism but there is an intriguing similarity in attitude.

There are three million Jains in the world today and virtually all of them live in India. Jains are divided into two distinct groups. The Digambaras are committed to the complete rejection of all possessions, including clothing. Digambaras monks are perpetually naked. They also do not admit women to their monastic orders. The Shvetambaras are more liberal in their approach. They permit their monks to wear simple white clothes; they also admit women to their monastic orders.

A distinctive Jain belief is the doctrine of *ahimsa*. For Jains *ahimsa* (non-injury) involves the conscious avoidance of all acts of injury and killing. It also implies a complete rejection of possession and consumption; consumerism and Jainism have very little in common! This doctrine of *ahimsa* has resulted in a number of distinctive Jain practices. This includes the monastic practice of carrying a small broom or whisk with which to brush aside any living creature before one sits or lies down. Some Jains wear a face mask over their mouths and noses; this practice stems from a desire to prevent the accidental ingestion of tiny insects. Jains are committed vegetarians. Jains are discouraged from all professions that might harm living creatures. For example few Jains are farmers; digging the ground might easily damage worms or snails.

The Jains are also firm believers in reincarnation. Indeed the Digambaras believe that it is impossible for women to gain salvation; they must first become men. The Jain understanding of karma is unusual. Unlike the Hindu, the Jain does not consider the material world to be an illusion. Like the gnostic, the Jain believes both in the reality and in the evil of the material realm. According to Jain philosophy bad karma is caused by the cloying presence of matter. Fine particles of matter can attach themselves to a soul and so prevent the soul from floating back up to heaven. Salvation means to cease reincarnation and to return to heaven as a spirit; all bodies and matter have vanished. Unlike Hinduism, but again like the gnostic position, the Jain soul retains its individuality.

Bad karma can only be eradicated by voluntary suffering. Self-imposed suffering is the perfect antidote to karmic bondage. As the Jain ascetic reaches old age, he or she may choose to die voluntarily, undertaking a ritual death by fasting. This is called *sallekhana*.

5. *The Gnostic Impact upon Christianity*

This attitude towards the material realm can sometimes creep into Christianity. In the film *The Rapture*, Mimi Rogers plays a woman who has become obsessed by the 'rapture'. When her husband is killed by a man who has run amok with a rifle, she takes her daughter into the desert. She believes that God will 'snatch her up' into heaven. Her daughter is very disappointed when this 'rapture' does not materialise and she becomes distraught. 'Mummy,' she screams, 'Why can't we go to heaven now? Why can't we just die?' Mimi Rogers decides to oblige. She buys a gun and shoots her own daughter. Unfortunately she is unable to finish off the job by killing herself!

Although fictional, this film conveys a gnostic attitude to life. Heaven is good and earth is bad. Why wait for heaven when you can commit suicide? There have even been missionaries in South America who have killed their recently-converted followers; the soul, they reasoned, must be immediately released from the evil body.

Conclusion

And all this brings us back to Simeon. Like Origen, like Marcion the gnostic and like the Jains, he believed that his true home was not earth but heaven! As the Orphic inscription, found in Petelia, declares: 'I am a child of earth and of the starry heaven/But heaven is my home.' Simeon, the Stylite, would have agreed with this.[3]

Notes

1. Will Durant, *The Age of Faith*, Vol 4 of *The Story of Civilisation* (Simon and Schuster: New York, 1950), p60.
2. A. H. Armstrong, *An Introduction to Ancient Philosophy* (Methuen: London, 1947), p6.
3. I am indebted to Armstrong's book for many of the ideas in this chapter. Albert Wolters has also contributed many insights.

Simeon Stylites

This story can be found at the beginning of this chapter.

For further thought

1. Why did Simeon live on a pillar for thirty-seven years?
2. What is the 'Orphic Myth'? How might this myth have influenced Simeon?
3. Why did some people worship Simeon?

The Albigensians

Theological orthodoxy has long been a vexed issue in the Christian church and the story of the Albigensians illustrates perfectly the dramatic consequences of a major theological conflict.

From the 12th century onward, heretical splinter groups became very numerous across Europe and precipitated a strong papal response. By 1199, Pope Innocent III was talking about heresy as a form of 'treason'.

By this time the Albigensians had spread widely in both France and Italy. The essence of their teaching was a belief in two gods, a good god who had created the invisible, spiritual world and an evil god who had created the visible, material world. Matter, including the human body, was evil and was controlled and directed by the evil god who was identified with the God of the Old Testament, Yahweh. This God had imprisoned the human soul in its earthly body; death would force this soul to find another body, animal or human. Redemption or salvation could only occur if this cycle of birth and rebirth were broken. Christ, the Son of the good god, had been sent by him to offer release and salvation to these tortured souls. This gnostic perspective led the Albigensians to deny the incarnation of Christ and his bodily resurrection.

The Albigensians believed in only one sacrament, which would enable the suffering soul to escape from the evil material world. This sacrament was called the *consolamentum* and was administered by the laying-on-of-hands. There were two grades of Albigensian. The Perfects who had received the *consolamentum* lived in strict poverty and ascetic renunciation. They fasted regularly, ate no meat and rejected marriage. Below them were the mere 'Believers' who venerated the Perfect and delayed receiving the sacrament until they were in danger of death.

In the first decade of the 13th century, Pope Innocent III unleashed the full fury of the Roman Catholic church against the Albigensians. It is said that half a million soldiers were gathered for the enterprise. The crusaders' advance was irresistible. Bezières and Carcasonne were at once besieged and the inhabitants indiscriminately massacred. In the first three months of the crusade, five hundred towns and fortresses fell or surrendered and amongst them the town Albi which has inspired the name – Albigensian. The conflict was continuous and brutal, even for a religious war. 'Slay all, God will know His own,' was the famous slogan of one famous ambassador.

At Lavaur, a leading lady was thrown into a well and stones rolled upon her. Eight hundred were hanged on trees or hewn in pieces. Four hundred of the 'perfect' were burned at the stake; the rest, men, women and children were massacred.

After the crusade, the Inquisition was established in 1231–33 to root out heresy by unstinting persecution. Confessed heretics were sometimes forced to wear special symbols that indicated their peculiar heresy. The unrepentant often suffered the fate of being burnt at the stake. By about 1245, the Albigensian community had ceased to exist.

For further thought

1. Who were the Albigensians? Outline their gnostic beliefs.
2. How were they persecuted?
3. What was the Inquisition?

Source: ed. John Henry Blunt, *Dictionary of Sects, Heresies, Ecclesiastical Parties and Schools of Religious Thought* (Longmans, Green and Co: London, 1891).

The Flagellants

During the 14th century the population of Europe was devastated by a painful and fatal disease that became known as the black death. Historians of the subsequent centuries have argued that the cause of this terrible plague involved polluted water supplies, tainted foodstuffs and the ubiquitous germ-laden black rat. The disease was characterised by large swellings in the groin and armpits and the emergence of dark growths on the skin's surface. For many fourteenth century people this plague was divine retribution for their many sins.

The tragedy of famine and plague can often be accompanied by the feverish hunt for a scapegoat. The black death proved to be no exception. In Germany it was popularly believed that Jews had been poisoning the wells. Many Jewish men and women were walled in their houses and left to starve. Some Jews were burnt alive. Lepers were also scapegoated; the fortunate ones were refused entry into the walled cities but many others were stoned to death.

In times of great crisis and uncertainty, bizarre and extreme movements can often flourish. Outstanding among these during the terrible days of the black death were the Flagellants. These fervent men and women marched through the cities of Europe in long processions, clad in mourning garments, with red crosses on their shirts, their eyes fixed to the ground. Purple banners and lighted candles would precede them in colourful and theatrical fashion; crowds would gather and welcome them with the ringing of bells.

As soon as the Flagellents had gathered in the main square of the city, they would begin their gruesome acts of contrition.

Singing penitential psalms, they would strip to the waist; both men and women. They would then lie down in different positions; the perjurers would hold up three fingers and the adulterers would lie face downwards. And then they would flog themselves with whips tipped with metal studs until the blood ran down to their feet. The pilgrimage would last for thirty-three days and each Flagellant would promise to flog himself or herself three times a day for the entire period. The leader of the sect would move among them and whip all those who lacked conviction in their self-mutilations.

Unfortunately, as the Flagellants moved from city to city they carried the plague with them. Not unexpectedly, public opinion was to turn against them. Indeed the Flagellant's public profile rapidly changed from hero to villain and they came under attack from many city dwellers. To add to their troubles they also attracted the attraction of the Inquisition and within a few years the sect was accused of heresy and many Flagellents were burnt at the stake. By the end of the fifteenth century the movement had disappeared.

For further thought

1. You have just become a Flagellant. What has lead you to join this movement?
2. The Flagellants have just arrived in your town. What do they do?
3. In what sense can we refer to the Flagellants as a gnostic movement?

Source: John Blunt, *Dictionary of Sects, Heresies, Ecclesiastical Parties and Schools of Religious Thought*, (Longman, Green and Co: London, 1891).

Ascetics

Ascetics are those rare people who practice rigorous self-discipline and self-denial. Some of the most committed of these people have been the Syrian monks who lived sixteen hundred years ago.

Everything that could reduce sleep and enhance discomfort was explored. In their monasteries Syrian monks would tie ropes around their bellies and were then suspended in an awkward position; some were tied to standing posts. One zealous monk exposed his naked body to poisonous flies while sleeping in a marsh for six months.

Personal hygiene was often neglected by committed ascetics. In the blazing heat of the desert, it required considerable self-control to refrain from the usual activities of bathing and washing. These austere types could be seen wandering around the wilderness with their long hair hanging in wild abandonment and dressed in rancid rags; their fingernails uncut, their bodies covered in dirt, dust and sweat.

Another ascetic practice, the reduction of movement, was popular with this unusual group. Complete seclusion in a tiny cell was believed to be extremely beneficial; solitary confinement in wildernesses, cliffs and mountains was also widely practised. Iron devices such as girdles and chains were placed around the loins, neck, hands and feet; these pain-inducing contraptions were sometimes hidden under their clothes. There have even been ascetics who have castrated themselves.

The Hindu fakirs of India provide the most astonishing examples of self-inflicted pain and suffering. Some stare at the sun until they go blind; others hold up their arms above their heads until they wither.

The gnostic attitude to life has inspired many men and women to undergo the most painful trials and tribulations.

For further thought

1. What is an 'ascetic'?
2. Outline the ascetic practices of the Syrian monks.
3. How can gnostic attitudes influence Christian behaviour?

Source: *The Encyclopedia Brittanica*. Article – 'Asceticism'.

The Shakers

Nathaniel was captivated by the sight before him. The wooden floors creaked as the assembled congregation arose to begin their religious dancing. As a newcomer to the community, Nathaniel was unsure of what to do. Before he could decide, he felt a hand grasp his firmly and pull him to his feet. It was Lucy, the young woman who had convinced him to join the community that she claimed was the Kingdom of God on earth. Slowly the worshippers formed into a circular pattern and chanted their unfamiliar songs. The tempo was rising with each verse and Nathaniel could feel his pulse racing with anticipation. Suddenly one of the throng fell to the floor and began shaking violently. Others quickly joined her and soon most of the gathering were shaking and singing with great joy on their faces. Nathaniel now understood why this new religious group was called the Shakers.

Such would have been a typical scene in the Shaker community which enjoyed its heyday in the late nineteenth century. The Shakers, a Christian group, believed that the Second Coming had taken place with the arrival of their leader Ann Lee who had immigrated to America in 1774. Based around Albany, New York, she established community villages, each of which was believed to be a part of the Garden of Eden. By 1850 there were over 6000 members in 18 Shaker villages. As their theology demanded celibacy and the expulsion of anyone found to be engaging in a sexual liaison, this growth was very impressive.

The Shakers believed in the equality of the sexes and the maintenance of a simple lifestyle. They encouraged quality craftsmanship and became world famous for the elegance and simplicity of their furniture. In fact, the Shaker, Tabitha Babbitt, was responsible for the invention of the circular saw, a tool which has become virtually indispensable in the art of furniture-making.

Given that the Shakers were celibate and therefore solely reliant on outside recruitment for the maintenance of their community, it comes as no surprise that they have all but disappeared from the face of the earth.

For further thought

1. Who were the Shakers?
2. How have gnostic ideas influenced this Christian movement?
3. What were some of the positive contributions of the Shaker community?

Brief Notes

The Shakers are a good example of religious syncretism. They combined gnostic with Christian ideas. It was very common for gnostic groups to forbid marriage. Sex and the body must be shunned.

Source: *Dictionary of Sects, Heresies, Ecclesiastial Parties and Schools of Religious Thought*, (Longmans, Green and Co: London, 1891).

Korean Fundamentalism

At precisely four o'clock in the afternoon of Wednesday 28th October 1992, the sky will be filled with a bright light. Jesus Christ will appear – initially in South Korea – with arms outstretched; and the Rapture will take place. . . . .

So went the predictions, biblically and mathematically calculated, of a small Korean called Tae-Young Kwon. Those who had led blameless lives, or had repented in time, would be transported to Heaven and eternal joy would be theirs. For those unfortunate enough to be left behind it would be like Hell on earth, worse than one could imagine.

Regardless of the slightly negative fact that October 28th 1992 came and went without a perceptible number of South Koreans inexplicably disappearing from the planet, Mr Kwon is not alone in preaching such predictions of the coming 'Rapture'. In South Korea more than 250 churches preach the same message based upon Mr Kwon's calculations, which he first published in 1979, and his Mission for the Coming Days organisation has branches all over the world.

Apocalyptic fervour grew apace in the months preceding the 28th October: businessmen were selling up, workers were leaving their jobs. One old lady spent weeks travelling the country, saying goodbye to relatives. A woman in Seoul was reported to have had an abortion because she was afraid that she might be too heavy to ascend to heaven.

Another colourful figure in Mr Kwon's Tami Church (*tami* is an abbreviation of the Korean for 'preparing for the coming future') is pastor Lee Jang Lim. He not only preaches about the 'Coming Day' to his noisy, excited congregation, he also reassures those who find themselves left behind on the fateful day. He gives detailed instructions on what to do if they find themselves at the mercy of the Antichrist – stay calm and do not panic!

Unfortunately some of Pastor Lee's followers have had their devotion to his message somewhat shaken. Just a month before the Rapture day he was arrested on suspicion of pocketing nearly £2.5 million of church donations. Not only that, he also held financial bonds that were not due until 1995 when, according to the predictions, money would be worthless.

On the wall of Pastor Lee's church hangs a graphic and lurid painting of what the day of Rapture will be like: Jesus hangs with outstretched arms high above Seoul's skyscrapers; believers float heavenward and on the ground all is chaos; cars go out of control as drivers are 'raptured' out of their vehicles, and airplanes crash crewless to the ground.

For further thought

1. What is meant by the term – 'The Rapture'?
2. How does this story illustrate a syncretism of Christian and gnostic belief?
3. How can belief in the rapture lead to an otherworldly understanding of Christianity?

Source: Peter Hillmore, *Observer* Magazine, (25th October, 1992).

ISLAM

INTRODUCTION

The passionate religion of Islam has been eloquently described in Bill Musk's book *Passionate Believing*. He has devised an imaginary conversation between three Muslim women which can help us to understand Islam:

> As Raihaneh walked with her friends towards home in the southern quarters of the busy capital, she joined in the hoarse conversation concerning Iran's enemy number one.
>
> 'How can those Western sluts point their finger at us, saying that we are being returned to medieval bondage? We women are secure in the path which the Lord has set out for us.'
>
> 'Yes,' interjected Ferri, 'The Qur'an and *sunna* set us free to be women as we should be. Not like those painted dolls that used to flaunt their Western 'freedom' around this city. The ones who knew they were women dressed like prostitutes, showing their pink flesh to every male eye. The others who dressed like men, who behaved like men, "equal this, equal that", they didn't even know that they were women with breasts!'
>
> 'Our families will see us securely married! We shall be able to fulfil our religion and produce children for our husbands.'
>
> 'Our way is the way of God. Can you imagine a society where a woman takes it upon herself to marry this one today, that one tomorrow?' asked Raihaneh.
>
> 'Or just to live with a partner and never marry?' interposed Pari.

'Can you imagine that? If ever a nation needed sharia law it is America!'

'No wonder their menfolk are so lost. They are born of a generation of prostitute mothers! Our Komitehs have cleaned out the red-light sore in our city; there is hope with God for the girls who sold their flesh there. But who can clean out a nation of adulterers?' harangued Raihaneh.

'Our leader is right when he calls that nation the Great Satan!'[1]

There are many Muslims today who would agree wholeheartedly with Raihaneh, Ferri and Pari. Why do they think this? Why are they so intolerant of America, the Great Satan?

Key Beliefs and Practices of Islam

1. Islam Rejects Western Consumerism

Many Muslims are very critical of the western attitude to life. They look at the consumerist west and they are deeply repelled. They perceive western consumerism as a corrupt and evil way of life.

For the consumerist, life can often boil down to an obsession with shopping, pleasure and profit. We are born. We grow up. We sow our wild oats. We make money. We consume goods and services. We watch films and football. We grow old. We die. The Muslim completely rejects this 'atheistic' perspective. Many Muslims are shocked by permissive, liberal attitudes to sex and marriage. They are also very surprised by western advertising that seems to encourage greed and lust. Drink coke and you will be happy. Buy this car and your romantic longings will be fulfilled. Wear this perfume and you will become a sexually attractive woman.

But it is not only this. The Muslim is persuaded that western consumerism is exporting its dubious values to the rest of the world. They look at a country like Thailand and they argue that this non-western country has become corrupted by western tourists and western materialism. Prostitution and poverty have spiralled in recent years in that sad country. The Muslim believes that the consumerist way of life is like a huge juggernaut that is hurtling down the motorway destroying everything in its way.

The Muslim waves his finger and points to America, the Great Satan. For many Muslims America seems to incarnate consumerism in its most lethal and developed form. America simply oozes that odious 'western' point of view. Perhaps now we can begin to understand these three Iranian women.

2. Islam believes in One God

Islam begins and ends with the confession that there is no God but Allah. Muhammad is the supreme prophet of Islam and he believed that God had commanded him to preach against the pagan religion of his native Arabia. The prophet urged his countrymen to give up their pagan idols and to turn to the true and only God, Allah. Islam is opposed to the worship of many gods and the pagan practice of idolatry.

At the same time Islam rejects the Hindu belief that God is everything and everything is God. Islam rejects both polytheism and pantheism. It is blasphemy to a Muslim if a human being claims to be god. A Hindu yogi who claims to be a god would receive no spiritual encouragement or sympathy from a committed Muslim. A Hindu might worship a cow, a rat or a cobra. From a Muslim perspective this would be blasphemy.

Not surprisingly there is a point of conflict between this aspect of Islam and the Christian faith. The Christian believes that God has become flesh in the person of Jesus Christ. The Muslim rejects all such talk and emphasises the unity of God. For a Muslim it is impossible for God to become a person.

Islam draws a clear distinction between the Creator and his creation. God is not what he has made. What he has made, he is not. This distinction is found also in Judaism and Christianity.

3. A Person is a vice-regent of Allah

Islam sees humanity as the creatures of Allah and subject to his will. Men and women exist in dependence upon Allah and are sustained by his power and wisdom. The purpose of life is to love, adore and serve Allah. Human beings are completely subject to the will of Allah; the very word 'Muslim' means one who is submitted to Allah.

The Muslim understands his task in life to be that of a vice-regent. He must rule the world on behalf of Allah. He is accountable to Allah for the world that has been entrusted to his care. This attitude to life contrasts strikingly with the gnostic or Orphic perspective. Islam is not an otherworldly religion; it is very much concerned with the here and now.

In response to this understanding of life, the Muslim is zealous to accomplish the will of Allah in all areas of life. The Islamic law or *sharia* embraces banking, politics, rates of taxation, the care of animals and livestock, economics, education, diet, social behaviour and family life. Islam can never be reduced to personal piety or personal morality. In Islam there is no split between secular and sacred; all of life belongs to Allah. For example the *sharia* is most emphatically opposed to usury (the charging of interest); this aspect of the sharia must be respected in both business and 'high finance'. At the same time Islam has a distinctive understanding of government and politics; a split between spiritual life and political life makes no sense to the committed Muslim.

4. The Five Pillars of Islam

It is within this broad context that Islam imposes particular disciplines upon the individual Muslim. These human responsibilities are essentially contained in the 'Five Pillars' of Islam:

1. **Shahada**. This is the Islamic confession of faith. It is a commitment to obey Allah and to follow the prophet Muhammed.

'I bear witness that there is no god but God; I bear witness that Muhammad is the Apostle of God.' These words are the first words spoken to a child at birth and the last words which a Muslim would utter with his dying breath.

2. **Salat**. Prayer is the second pillar of Islam. There are five prayer times, each preceded by ritual washing – dawn, midday, mid-afternoon, sunset, and night. These prayers remind Muslims in a regular and disciplined manner of their duties and responsibilities to Allah.

3. **Zakat**. The Muslim must share part of his wealth with the poor and needy, the debtor and the prisoner. The sharia is meticulous in determining the amounts of alms which should be given on different categories of possessions. Contemporary practice has simplified the matter to an annual rate of $2\frac{1}{2}$ per cent of one's cash balance.

4. **Sawm**. Fasting is the fourth pillar of Islam. During the month of Ramadan, Muslims must abstain from food and drink through the daylight hours of the entire month, from early dawn to sunset. In a hot country this can be a very demanding discipline.

5. **Hajj**. Once in a Muslim's life a person is expected to make a pilgrimage to the holy city of Mecca. In this city a Muslim can find many 'memorials' of the Islamic past. There are many associations with the prophet Muhammed who began his life and ministry in Mecca.

5. Additional laws

The sharia contains some very strict laws. For example the law prescribes the death penalty for a Muslim who abandons his faith. The technical term for this is apostasy. The sharia also prescribes the death penalty for any Muslim who is caught in adultery. For certain acts of theft, the sharia prescribes amputation of the hand; and for drunkenness severe flogging is required. Committed Muslims are not allowed to drink alcohol and they are forbidden to eat pork.

6. Jihad

The word *jihad* means literally 'extraordinary effort' or 'great striving for Allah'. Because this effort or striving is nowhere more strenuous than in war, jihad came to mean holy war. The basic idea of *jihad* comes from the Qu'ran. Here is a passage from chapter 8, *The Spoils*: 'Let not Unbelievers think that they can get away from us, the Godly (ie Muslims). Muster against them all the men at your disposal so that you may strike terror into the enemies of Allah.'

Jihad can be fought using military, economic and political means. *Jihad* can be declared against all those who are considered to be enemies of Allah; this can sometimes mean that one Muslim country will wage *jihad* against another Muslim country. For example during the Iran/Iraq war the Iranians claimed that they were waging holy war against their Iraqi neighbours.

The aim of *jihad* is always to bring the non-Muslim world and the corrupt Muslim world under the dominance of faithful Islam.

7. The Last Day

The Qu'ran teaches that Allah will one day judge the world and all its inhabitants. At a moment known only to Allah, all people will be raised from the dead and face God's judgement. Islam, like Judaism and Christianity, embraces the biblical idea of the resurrection of the body; the whole person rises to face God. This teaching emphatically rejects the Orphic or Hindu belief in reincarnation. In Islam people live once and then they face judgement.

Allah will consign all people either to heaven or hell as He wills. Heaven or Paradise is conceived in the Qu'ran as a place of everlasting, sensual delight. A spring is constantly bubbling and around it are sumptuous chairs; beautiful carpets and magnificent ornaments are everywhere. It is here that the righteous servants of Allah can relax and enjoy themselves;

exquisite wine and fresh spring water abound; fruit and grapes are there for the picking. The open square of Paradise is surrounded by attractive, shade-providing trees. The men who attain this paradise will enjoy the company of dark-eyed virgins (houris) to whom Allah has granted eternal youth.

In sharp contrast, the damned will be banished to hell, forever separated from God. The wicked are promised everlasting fiery torment. Those who cry out for relief will receive the 'comfort' of scalding water.

Islamic narratives contain many references to the profound and passionate wish of the early Muslims to reach this paradise as soon as possible. The Qu'ran teaches that all those who die a martyr's death will gain immediate entry to paradise and there have been many Muslims who have sought this premature death firm in the belief that paradise would be their reward.

Islam is a very powerful force in our world today. Some observers believe that there will be at least one billion followers of Islam by the year 2000.

Notes

1. Bill A. Musk, *Passionate Believing* (Monarch: Tunbridge Wells 1992), p148.

Muhammad

Muhammad was born into the Kuraish tribe in the city of Mecca about 570 AD. The Kuraish, who were dominant in Mecca at the time, were commercially very successful, and had made Mecca a prosperous city and established it as a leading trade centre in the Middle East. It was also famous as a pagan centre with religious life revolving around a small temple called the Kaba. It attracted a host of pilgrims from the various Arabic tribes who came to worship their gods of wood and stone. As well as being loyal to their many gods, the Arabs at this time were fiercely loyal to their tribes. Blood ties were held to be sacred and tribal honour had to be defended at all costs, thus Muhammad also grew up in a culture of blood feuding and tribalism.

As Muhammad's parents died when he was young, he was raised by relatives. Upon reaching adulthood, he had not accumulated enough capital to establish himself as a merchant so he found employment with a wealthy widow, Khadija instead. He quickly impressed her with his commercial ability and they eventually married.

Important though his business life was, Muhammad also spent at least one month a year meditating in a cave. It was during one of these periods of meditation that he was to have a profound religious experience. It seems that he was visited in his sleep by the angel Gabriel and ordered to recite! Confused at first, Muhammad followed the instruction and found himself reciting words. The experience was repeated numerous times and Muhammad eventually realized that there was only one god, Allah, and that he was to be his messenger.

Initially he was uneasy about revealing the details of this new revelation but after three years he began to proclaim publicly that there was only one God, before whom all must appear at the end for judgement. Although Muhammad was not well received in Mecca, he slowly accumulated some followers and established Islam as a way of life. He demanded that his followers worship Allah only, pray five times a day, and abstain from theft, fornication and blood feuding.

Muhammad became increasingly unpopular as he disparaged the local pagan gods. Hostility grew to the point where he was forced to leave Mecca. Fortunately he was offered the post of leadership in the city of Medina to the north and he set off on the journey which is now referred to as 'the Hegira'.

Muhammad quickly gained control of Medina and decided to wage a holy war against Mecca. After eight years of military struggle he forced the surrender of his former city and entered it as its triumphant leader. Without hesitation, Muhammad purged the sanctuary of its pagan idols and set himself the task of detailing the Muslim rite of pilgrimage. Based upon his revelations in the cave, Muhammad wrote the Qu'ran which he completed by AD 631. He thereby laid the foundation for the Muslim faith we see today and died a year later in AD 632.

For further thought

1. Why were the merchants of Mecca opposed to the new teachings of Muhammad?
2. What aspects of 'pagan' Mecca did Muhammad condemn? Why?
3. Find out all you can about the Muslim rite of pilgrimage.

Source: *The World's Religions* No single author (Lion: Tring, Hertfordshire, 1982).

Muslims in Bolton

Arthur and Hilary Jones had been living in Bolton for several years and were both involved in community relations work with the Church of England. The Manchester diocese had employed them to build and foster healthy relationships between Asian and British people. In Bolton there is a large Asian population and many of these Asian people are Muslim.

The extended family is a very noticeable feature of such Asian communities. Some forty to fifty members of the same family, grandparents, aunts, uncles, fathers, mothers and children often live very closely and intimately together. Such people often prefer the old terraced housing that is a common sight in a northern city like Bolton.

Arthur and Hilary were very impressed with the strong communal ties of the many Muslims that they met. Unlike English people who tend to buy property for a particular individual or couple, Asian people often club together and buy a house for the entire extended family. If a young man marries a young woman, his extended family will pool resources and purchase an appropriate property for the new couple. Mortgages are seldom required and a great deal of money is not wasted on interest payments!

In 1990, during the Christmas holidays, Arthur and Hilary were saddened to hear that Arthur's 75 year-old father had been knocked over by a bus. The shock of the accident and the severity of the bruises proved fatal and the funeral was speedily arranged. Hilary and Arthur informed their Asian friends of this sad event.

Several days later, one of the leading men in the local

extended family dropped into Arthur and Hilary's for a cup of tea. He had brought a superb basket of fruit – enough for several weeks – and a small gift. He was very concerned for the Joneses and expressed his sadness at the sudden death of Arthur's father.

Arthur and Hilary were very surprised when their guest offered to lend them a large loan (£1000) interest free. The Asian man explained that he knew how expensive funerals could be and was very concerned that money should not be a burden at such a difficult time.

Hilary and Arthur did not need the money but they were delighted to have such sensitive and thoughtful neighbours.

For further reflection

1. Why did the Muslim man offer to lend the Joneses a large loan *interest free*?
2. How is the Islamic understanding of family life different from the British understanding?
3. You are a member of a large extended Muslim family. Describe your life.

Brief Notes

In Islam there is a very strong emphasis upon the family and in particular the extended family. Islam does not encourage hedonism and individualism. The Koran is most emphatic that 'usury' is immoral and this would explain the interest-free loan.

Ginger

Ginger was an attractive student at the University of California in Los Angeles. Like many Americans, she mixed freely with men, chatted in an animated way, smiled frequently, and would occasionally touch a male companion on the arm in the course of conversation.

Ginger and Ali met in class. He was a Muslim from a high government family in Iran. Ginger and Ali were attracted to one another. Ginger noted immediately that Ali was different from most American men. He was more considerate, sensitive and gentle. Eventually he asked her for a date. Their first evening together was pleasant for both of them. Other dates followed and the level of intimacy grew deeper. When Ali asked Ginger to marry him, she already felt so committed that she could not say no.

Ali talked to Ginger about his religion. He told her about his belief in God, and in Christ as a prophet, how the Qu'ran taught about Jesus' birth by the Virgin Mary, and his miracles of healing and raising people from the dead. He also told her that Muslims believed in all the prophets and in the Holy Books.

Ginger's parents assented to their marriage. 'After all,' they said, 'they both believe in the same God and in Jesus and the Holy Books, and that's enough.'

Ginger and Ali were married and had their first child in the United States before they returned to his homeland. Upon arriving in Iran, Ginger's passport was taken away, and she was told now that she was the property of her husband. Shortly after, she was cruelly shocked when she learned that Ali already had a wife. Ali assumed that Ginger would understand that Muslims were allowed to have more than one wife. He could not understand why she was so upset. Ginger became more unhappy when she learned that Muslims did not really believe in the deity of Christ, or his ability to forgive people's sins.

Feeling culturally isolated and religiously betrayed, Ginger began to agitate for her return to the United States. Her husband was willing to allow her to leave Iran and said that he would be happy to give her a certificate of divorce. However, she would have to leave her child behind in Iran. Ginger was trapped; in order to regain her passport she would have to forfeit her marriage and her child.

For further thought

1. Imagine that you are Ginger and you have just discovered that Ali is already married. What might you write in your diary?
2. What aspects of Islam can we learn about from this story?
3. In what ways do Christianity and Islam conflict with each other in this story?

Source: This story was told to us by a teacher living in Jerusalem.

Dietary Considerations

George Fanshaw worked in a large engineering firm which employed overseas nationals. In the course of time, George became good friends with Saleh Abdullah al-Fokra. George and his wife, Ann, invited Saleh home to a meal.

Later in the evening, during the meal, Saleh commented on how tasty the beef dish was. Ann remarked, 'Oh, thank you! This is one of my new recipes for beef bourguignonne. It has beef, lean bacon, carrots and onions plus a little red wine.' At this, Saleh became very upset and visibly ill. He asked to be taken outdoors as he felt he was going to become sick. George escorted him to the bathroom at which point Saleh threw up into the wash basin.

George felt angry but did manage to help Saleh to clean himself up. Saleh was both angry and embarrassed. He explained that he had never eaten bacon nor had ever drunk any wine in his life since both were forbidden to those who worshipped God. He didn't know whether to be angry at those who had betrayed him in this way or to apologise for creating such a bad impression on his host and hostess. After a few minutes of awkward conversation, Saleh said that he didn't feel well and asked permission to leave.

After Saleh had left, there were sharp words between Ann and George. 'I don't ever want to see one of those foreign friends of yours again,' she snapped. 'What a stupid religion that is anyway! And who is going to clean up that mess in the bathroom?'

For further thought

1. Why was Saleh so upset?
2. 'The Sharia contains some very strict laws.' Discuss.
3. Saleh has returned home after this embarrassing evening. What might he write in his diary?

Source: This true story was told to us by a teacher living in Jerusalem.

Why Was He Smiling?

It was a warm October morning in 1983 and the American marines on sentry duty outside their barracks in Beirut were hoping for a quiet morning. When a run-down old Lebanese truck approached the gate, they were not unduly alarmed; the driver seemed very happy. He was smiling.

Suddenly, to their surprise, the truck picked up speed, jinked between some barrels set up as a barrier and accelerated towards the five-story building behind them. As the truck crashed into the building, a massive explosion tore through the complex. 241 marines were killed.

The marines on duty were lucky enough to survive the attack and were appalled at what they had seen. They had seen the driver's face just before his death. Bemused and dazed, they repeatedly murmured; 'But the guy was smiling, the guy was smiling. Jeez, a guy doesn't smile when he knows he's going to die . . . . . does he?'

A week later a curious journalist set up a meeting with the leader of the Shi'a Islamic fundamentalist group responsible for the killing. The calm, composed leader explained to the journalist the reason for the suicide mission, 'It is really very simple, we are at war with the Americans, who are the enemies of Allah.'

Gingerly, the journalist asked the question that was burning in his mind – 'Why was the suicide attacker smiling as he went to certain death?'

'Because he was also going to equally certain paradise. Having killed enemies of Allah he became a martyr beloved by Allah. Of course he was smiling.'

Pressing his point, the interviewer asked – 'Would you drive a truck bomb and blow yourself up with it?'

'Of course. Death in the name of Islamic holy war is the purest form of sacrifice.'

'How long is this holy war likely to last?' probed the journalist.

'Until all the enemies of Islam are overcome, one way or another. The Holy Koran promises that this will happen but it may take years.'

For further thought

1. Why was this man smiling?
2. What is meant by the Islamic term – '*jihad*'?
3. What is a martyr?

Source: John Laffin, *Holy War: Islam Fights* (Grafton Books: London, 1988).

THE NEW AGE MOVEMENT

INTRODUCTION

In his book *Disarming the Secular Gods* Peter Moore tells the following story about a young sixteen-year-old boy. Johnny has been thinking about his recent confirmation and he decides to get 'unconfirmed'. He telephones his mother and asks the following question:

> 'Hi, mum. How do you get unconfirmed?'
> The mother did what any parent would do under the circumstances. She asked for clarification.
> 'Why, Johnny, what do you mean?'
> 'How do you get unconfirmed?' he said. 'You see, I've been walking around the grounds and woods here with a friend, and he's helping me to come up with a whole new viewpoint. God is really *in* nature. He's in the trees, the rocks, the sky and the birds. Mum, I just can't believe in that heavenly Father bit any more. I want to be unconfirmed!'[1]

Why did Johnny want to be 'unconfirmed'? To understand Johnny and his decision, we will need to unravel the mysteries of the 'New Age movement'.

The New Age movement is something of an enigma. We hear of New Age travellers and a New Age fascination with crystals and tarot cards. How can we make sense of all this?

169

Key Beliefs of the New Age Movement

1. The New Age is Eclectic

The New Age movement can be described as a syncretism or mixture of pagan, Hindu, Buddhist, Christian and secular ideas. It can be very difficult to pin down! A New Ager might embrace a smorgasbord of Celtic, Hindu and socialist beliefs.

One essential theme, however, can be said to characterise the New Age message. Nature is not a machine to be conquered and exploited. The world is not 'brute matter', denuded of purpose and value. One commentator has suggested that 'a flight from the secular worldview' is common to all so-called New Agers. This is probably correct.

2. All is One

The New Age perspective is pantheistic. Pantheism is the doctrine that the whole universe is God. We might even say that every part of the universe is a manifestation of God. Everything is one vast, interconnected process which is simply divine. New Agers speak about 'universal energy' and 'life force'.

Some New Agers refer to the world as a 'planetary being'. New Ager Stuart Wilson explains as follows:

> In this perception man is seen not as the exploiter and conqueror of Nature, but as an integral part of the Web, with the individual as a living cell within the greater Whole. Thus only the harmony of the individual with the Whole can benefit the individual, and if we are violent to any part of the Web we are ultimately violent to ourselves.
>
> This shifts the focus from a Web of Consciousness to a Web of Being – not a mere reflection of above into below, but a total interconnectedness and absolute integration. In this perception we begin to see the Earth as a conscious, struggling, living Being, with the oceans and rivers as its veins and arteries, the soil as its skin, and the forests as its lungs.
>
> This Planetary Being, which has been given many names including Gaia, is the system within which we live and move, the environment which nourishes and sustains us.[2]

A contrast at this juncture might prove helpful. The consumerist tends to perceive the world as a stockpile of raw materials that can be exploited. Trees, rivers and mountains can make you wealthy if you can subdue them and tap their economic potential. The New Ager recoils at this attitude to 'nature'. For the New Ager, those same trees, rivers, lakes and mountains are part of a living, pulsating Being 'Gaia', Mother Earth. Nature is not a machine; she is a living, divine being.

3. Humans Are Part of God

The premise that all is one leads to the conclusion that humanity is part of God/Gaia. People are part of the divine because the whole universe is God. 'I am God,' shouts influential New Ager Shirley MacLaine.

Humans are intrinsically divine beings. People, like everything else, are only extensions of the Planetery Being – Gaia. Humanity is not made up of millions of individual men and women. Individuality is really an illusion; we are all part of a cosmic oneness. This teaching is very similar to the teaching of the Upanishads which we encountered in our chapter on Hinduism. Shirley MacLaine has presented very similar 'pantheistic' ideas in her bestselling books.

4. But Most of Us Are Not Enlightened

According to the New Age perspective, most of the human race is ignorant of its divine origin. We have forgotten that we are part of Gaia. We live in a world of pain, tension, injustice and ecological catastrophe because we have lost touch with Gaia and her pulsating energy. This lack of enlightenment activates in us a brutality and cruelty towards ourselves, our neighbours and the plant and animal kingdoms. We have become alienated and cut off from each other and the planet earth. In short we are impoverished and unenlightened beings; foolish creatures who are enslaved by destructive lusts and avaricious longings. We perceive trees and rivers as something other than us, external objects to be used and abused. We fail to understand that we and nature are one.

5. Reincarnation

A common belief in the New Age movement is reincarnation. A lack of enlightenment will engender bad karma; this in turn will force anxious, brooding souls to leave and re-enter countless bodies, animal and human. Successive incarnations will provide endless possibilities to gain enlightenment. This belief in reincarnation assumes a 'western' focus in the New Age movement; it is no longer a curse but offers further opportunities to rediscover Gaia. Most New Agers do not approve of the caste system and its intrinsic inequalities. The western preoccupation with equality infuses New Age thinking.

6. Solution? We Must Reown Our Divinity

How do we dispel this ignorance and lack of enlightenment? The New Ager urges humankind to become enlightened and tune in to the hidden and occult life-force of Gaia. We need to shape up and return to Gaia. How can this be achieved? The new Ager is convinced that this return to our divine origin can be achieved by 'spiritual technology'. Elliot Miller explains as follows:

> New Agers believe that specific techniques for *altering* the consciousness (for example, meditation, chanting, ecstatic dancing, sensory deprivation) can enable the seeker to consciously (mystically) experience his (or her) supposed oneness with God. Thus, salvation for the New Ager is equated with *gnosis* (experiential knowledge). It is self-realization or the realization that one's true Self is God. Such mystical experiences are viewed as doorways to 'personal transformation' – a lifelong growth process marked by increasing wholeness and personal power.[3]

All kinds of mystical experiences can 'enlighten' our

consciousness and reorient us to our unity with Gaia. In this quest many New Agers avail themselves of 'occultic' experiences; these can include 'contacting the dead', 'automatic writing' and 'channelling'.

The occult practice of 'channelling' has become popular in many New Age circles. Channelling can be best described as a form of spiritualism. An example of channelling will be instructive. Jane Roberts, a poet from New York, was one day writing a poem. Suddenly she had a mystical experience; her thought-life changed dramatically and she felt inundated by new ideas and fresh visions. This experience activated in her a deep desire to investigate psychic activity. She and her husband experimented with an Ouija board and after a few sessions, the pointer spelled out messages that claimed to come from a personality called Seth.

This unseen, 'supernatural' being began to expound on religious, metaphysical and astrological subjects. Every week Jane would go into a deep trance and her husband would write down Seth's philosophical musings. This material was later published as two books, *The Seth Material* and *Seth Speaks*.

The basic message of Seth would seem to be that 'you create your own reality.' Many New Agers have been 'turned on' by this teaching; the Seth writings have attracted a readership numbering in the millions.[4]

Flotation tanks are common currency among some New Agers. You enter a small tank, filled with salty water; you close the door and suddenly there is pitch darkness. For many these flotation tanks can function as a relaxation technique; for others this 'sensory deprivation' can induce mystical experiences.

For many New Agers, hope for the world is intimately connected to mass enlightenment. Mystical experiences are crucial as we rediscover our unity with Gaia.

7. *This Enlightenment Will Transform the World*

Unlike the story of the yogi in our chapter on Hinduism, many New Agers are life-affirming and very much concerned with life here and now. It would be unfair to claim that the New Age movement is otherworldly. Astrological reflection is common currency among New Agers and there has emerged a distinctive understanding of a dawning Aquarian age.

New Agers are very concerned about the many threats to global survival. They point to acid rain, Chernobyl and the ozone layer and they are understandably alarmed. Unlike nihilism, the New Age movement offers an optimistic attitude to the future. They believe that a critical mass of transformed individuals can take responsibility for society as a whole and bring about *planetary transformation*.

According to the New Age astrological interpretation, we have passed through a destructive Piscean age of mass ignorance. Sometimes this age is equated with the dominance of the Christian religion; Pisces is the twelfth sign of the zodiac and evokes the idea of fish. The symbol of the fish is often associated with Christianity but we are now witnessing the dawning of the age of Aquarius. This zodiacal constellation is associated with water; in short the fish (Pisces) is being replaced by water (Aquarius) and this heralds a new age of ecological harmony and peace.

This teaching of a new age is intimately connected to a distinctive understanding of evolution. For the New Ager evolution is not based on random mutation and natural selection *à la* Darwin. Evolution is not grounded in chance but rather in purpose. Unseen, occult forces are leading the evolution of the planet into a new, more positive age. This understanding of evolution is derived from western secular sources; the Enlightenment belief in 'Progress' is very prominent. Humankind is progressively improving, morally, socially and ecologically.

Perhaps it should be pointed out at this juncture that Hinduism and pagan religions do not rhapsodise about a wonderful *future*. This is a secular idea grafted in with Hindu and pagan ideas.

We can now make more sense of Johnny's desire to get 'unconfirmed'. He has been exposed to New Age ideas and these ideas activated in him a distaste for more conventional religious ideas.

Notes

1. Peter Moore, *Disarming the Secular Gods* (Inter-Varsity Press: Leicester, 1989), pp35–36.
2. Stuart Wilson, *A Guide to the New Age* (Wayseeker Books: Exeter, 1989), p39.
3. Elliot Miller, *A Crash Course on the New Age Movement* (Monarch: Eastbourne, 1989), p17.
4. *Ibid* pp147–148. I am indebted to Elliot Miller for many of the ideas in this chapter.

Unconfirmed

Read the story about Johnny at the beginning of this chapter.

For further thought

1. What is pantheism? Relate this to the New Age idea of Gaia.
2. Imagine you are Johnny. You have been asked to write a letter to your bishop to explain why you wish to be 'unconfirmed'.
3. 'The New Age movement completely rejects consumerism'. Discuss.

Crystals

Harmonic Convergence Day was celebrated on August 16, 1987 by about 20,000 New Age devotees who travelled to 'sacred sites' all over the globe to participate in this cosmic event. On the Hawaiian island of Kauai, it was marked by the installation of a sacred crystal, known as 'Earthkeeper' because of its mystical powers of protection and knowledge, in the San Marga temple. According to a resident monk, this stone's destiny is to be adored as the naturally formed manifestation of the god Shiva.

This sacred crystal had its origins deep within the Quachita Mountains of Arkansas. It had been discovered by Jimmy Coleman in 1972. Viewing the perfectly formed, milky white quartz beauty which stood thirty nine inches high and weighed seven hundred pounds, Coleman sensed that it had a mysterious destiny. Thus he brought it to the surface and stored it without apparently having told anyone of its existence.

In July 1987, Almitra Zion, a Hindu scout from Kauai, arrived in Arkansas in search of a crystal which she said she had seen in a vision. Upon discovering Coleman's gigantic quartz, she convinced him to sell it to her group and had it transported to Hawaii. 'Earthkeeper', now enshrined in its temple, is being perpetually 'sanctified' by the light of a laser beam focused upon it. Worshippers come to receive the vibrations of the crystal and thereby to tune in to themselves and the cosmos.

It is believed that by tuning in to the vibrations of the crystal, one is in touch with mystical powers which can bring harmony and balance to the universe. Because crystals serve as good energy transmitters in electronics, it is assumed that they can transmit psychic or spiritual energy as well. Now many people, including such famous ones as the actress Shirley Maclaine possess their own crystals believing that they will help to bring them health, prosperity and peace of mind.

For further thought

1. Why are crystals so popular among New Agers?
2. What is meant by the technical term 'spiritual technology'?
3. In what sense may the New Age movement be described as eclectic?

Source: Russell Chandler, *Understanding the New Age* (Word (UK) Ltd: Milton Keynes, 1988).

Earth First

The residents of the valley overlooked by the Glen Valley Canyon Dam had a rude shock recently when they woke to see a long black crack working its way down the face of the dam. Fortunately for them, it was only a roll of black plastic, daringly unfurled by 'ecological warriors' Earth First!

Earth First's motto is: 'No compromise in defence of Mother Earth. Certainly their track record of spiking trees with large nails, disabling bulldozers, toppling survey stakes and felling power lines represents a vivid testimony to their commitment. Their manifesto proclaims that:

> We do not believe it is enough to preserve some of our remaining wilderness. We need to preserve it all, and it is time to recreate vast areas of wilderness in all of America's eco-systems, to close roads, remove developments and re-introduce extirpated wildlife.

They hold that many environmental groups are part of the establishment, committed to a human-centred outlook based on industrial progress. They view them as anti-Earth, anti-woman and anti-liberty.

Earth First's key skill is that of media manipulation. Madcap, daring schemes grab the media's attention and earn prime-time slots on television and front page newspaper headlines. In one campaign they gathered together forty protesters to climb the trees in an area of old growth forest in Portland. There they brandished banners daubed with 'Give a hoot – save the spotted owl.' The response was immediate. The timber corporation rose to the challenge and sent in their public relations consultants to confront them. This gave them the credibility that was crucial to the campaign.

Yet the credibility of the group is often stretched to breaking point by their commitment to bringing back the wilderness. With considerable cartographical confidence, Earth First has produced a map of the United States showing which third of it should be closed to human activity and cleansed of man's presence. While this vision is hardly likely to come to fruition, it has to be said that Earth First has scored some notable successes. Perhaps most notable of all is the formal declaration of the spotted owl as an endangered species.

For further thought

1. In what sense do 'Eco-guerillas' worship nature?
2. Compare and contrast New Age and consumerist approaches to nature.
3. What might be the attitude of Earth First to the Aids epidemic?

Brief Notes

In a consumerist worldview industrial progress is a key process. Man has only to conquer 'nature' and universal happiness will abound. Eco-guerillas reverse this commitment. Earth First believes that industrial progress is an unequivocal evil. Man and his progress are the enemies of nature. Man should not conquer nature; he should bow down and worship nature. (See section 1 of this chapter.)

To achieve this goal, some eco-guerillas are prepared to spike trees in order to harm those who would damage nature. They would say that trees are more important than environmentally destructive people.

Source: *The Guardian* (August 17, 1990).

Channelling

In the early 1950's three sociologists planted observers in a new group that was growing around a woman, based in Utah, who claimed to be a communicator with forces from another planet.

The woman, whom they dubbed 'Marian Keech' (to protect her identity), believed that she had received an initial message from her late father. Thereafter she waited patiently and allowed other forces to conduct her in automatic writing. 'Higher forces' from the planets Clarion and Cerus moved swiftly to establish a channel of communication with her. One 'supernatural being', Sananda communicated regularly and 'informed' her that he had been Jesus Christ in a previous life.

However, Marian was not inclined to publicise these messages and it was only after some enthusiastic members of other UFO groups heard about her contacts that a press release was issued in August 1954. Replete with obscure philosophical pronouncements, it also contained predictions of a cataclysmic disaster. Gradually the 'higher forces' revealed that a flood would wipe out Salt Lake City.

Mrs Keech decided to name her communicators the 'Guardians' and she received assurances from them that if she and her followers would gather together at the right time and place they would be rescued from the flood by flying saucers.

A date was set by the Guardians for the impending flood. The group members began to give up their jobs, possessions and friends and adopted strange and exotic diets. The 'Guardians' also required the removal of all metallic objects; rings, glasses and zippers were discarded.

Sadly, on the day in question, no flood came and no flying

saucers. The group became disillusioned and eventually disintegrated.

For further thought

1. What is meant by the New Age term 'channelling'?
2. Why was Mirian Keech so reluctant to reveal any details of her encounter with 'higher forces'?
3. How might dissatisfaction with a consumerist way of life lead to an interest in channelling?

NIHILISM

INTRODUCTION

There is an intriguing contrast between the world of punk rock and the world of the hippy rock star. Johnny Rotten, the lead singer of the notorious Sex Pistols, was contemptuous of all hippies. 'They were so complacent,' he said. 'They let the drug culture flop around them. They were so dosed out of their heads the whole time. Yeah man. Peace and love! Don't let anything affect you!'[1]

What made Rotten so disenchanted with the hippy scene? Many hippies had come to believe that the world's problems could be solved by a magical substance known as LSD. They came to believe that this chemical substance could create a world of peace and harmony. This hope, this optimisim, Rotten despised.

Many religions have maintained that the taking of hallucinogenic drugs is crucial to the healing of the world. The Aztec Indians used psilocybin during their all night festivals, believing that it enabled them to journey to the ends of the world. In shamanistic religions today, the shaman (a form of high priest who deals with the spirits on behalf of the tribe) will use both drugs and music to gain access to the spirit world.

LSD had been discovered during the war by a Swiss biochemist who had been experimenting with rye fungi. From the fifties onwards Americans began to imbibe this wonder-drug and discovered new and wacky worlds. In 1962 very few people had tried LSD; in 1971 it was estimated that five million Americans had 'tripped out on acid'. Without doubt, flowerpower types enjoyed the novelty and wildness of this new drug. Eventually there were those who came to appreciate the religious significance of LSD.

Timothy Leary, a famous dabbler in 'acid', became an ardent evangelist for the saving power of the drug. Leary believed that humans could begin to evolve into a near-perfect state if they blissed out regularly on the chemical saviour. Hippies began to entertain the idea that LSD could cleanse your mind of all evil and destructive desires. A 'tab' could cause a person to 'cosmically vibrate' and return that person to a state of gentle and childlike innocence.

The hippy world began to speak of love, peace and harmony. In 1967, Paul McCartney declared:

> The need today is for people to come to their senses and my point is that LSD can help them. We all know what we would like to see in the world today – peace. We want to be able to get on with each other. I believe the drug could heal the world . . . I now believe the answer to everything is love.[2]

This provocative panacea was taken very seriously by many intelligent people. Indeed, some suggested that the water systems of major cities should be spiked with the drug and so usher in a drug-induced utopia.

Sadly this optimism in LSD did not last long. Stories began to circulate of those who had 'blissed out' but whose minds never returned. They became known as acid casualties. There were also those whose trip activated in them the belief that they could fly. Like superman they hurled themselves out of windows. Unlike the man of steel, they crashed to the ground.

We have already seen how communists believe that the

revolution will bring a perfect world. We have investigated the Nazi faith in the Führer and now we can understand the faith of the hippy movement. Cosmically vibrate on acid and ye shall be saved!

How might a nihilist respond to all this hopeful talk? A nihilist is a person who rejects all suggestions of hope. Faith in revolution? Daft. Faith in the Führer? Ridiculous. Faith in LSD? Absurd. There is no hope. The word 'nihilist' comes from a Latin word and it means 'nothing'. A nihilist is a person who believes in 'nothingness'.

This is exactly the position that Johnny Rotten epitomizes so perfectly. Rotten portrayed himself as lazy, selfish and 'vacant'. In interviews he presented himself as a 'jaded youth, fed up with sex, cynical of love and happy to amuse himself by stubbing out lighted cigarettes on the back of his hand.' He once declared that: 'They try to ruin you from the start. They take away your soul. They destroy you. You have no future. Nothing.'[3]

This statement encapsulates the nihilist attitude to life. There is no purpose to life. There is no future; there is no hope. It is no wonder that Rotten sneered at the hippy 'flowerpot' optimism; Rotten would sneer at any position that offered hope!

Key Beliefs of Nihilism

1. The World is an Absurd Accident

The nihilist believes that the world is a tragic accident. There is no purpose and no meaning. The world is a sad product of evolutionary chance. Bertrand Russell, the famous philosopher, conveyed this belief very clearly: 'Such, in outline, but even more purposeless, more void of meaning, is the world which Science presents for our belief.'[4]

Russell, although he himself could not be described as a nihilist, believed that science had revealed that the world is purposeless and void of meaning. What does Russell mean by this? A contrast might prove helpful. For a Marxist, the world is not purposeless because Marx believed that the goal of history would be the establishing of a communist paradise. For Marx, the day will come when the working class will rise up and take control of all wealth and property. There is a future and there is a hope. The nihilist rejects this idea. The world has no purpose; it is void of meaning.

2. *Humans are Futile Wretches.*

The contemporary artist Francis Bacon believed that women and men are futile wretches: 'Also, man now realizes that he is an accident, that he is a completely futile being, that he has to play out the game without reason.'[5]

The French thinker Jean-Paul Sartre believed that because God does not exist, life has no ultimate meaning and is absurd. Sartre concluded that 'Man is a useless passion'. The famous playwright Samuel Beckett conveyed this attitude to life in his play *Breath*. The play lasts thirty seconds and there are no actors or conversation. The whole script is the sigh of human life from a baby's cry to a man's last breath before he dies.

This nihilist attitude to life is becoming increasingly pervasive today and can even lead to suicide! The writer Ernest Hemingway believed that 'Life is a rough track leading from nowhere to nowhere'.

On 2nd July 1961, Hemmingway shot himself with a shotgun. He blew away his entire cranial vault.

3. *The World is filled with Horror, Death and Misery*

The nihilist is overwhelmed with the horror and brutality of life on planet earth. Each evening as we turn on our television sets we are reminded that wars, famine, disease, terrorism, pollution, rape, murder and a host of vicious problems plague our world.

A darker side to science and technology seems to be emerging day by day. Napalm is a clever chemical that will burn you and yet not go out. An electrical appliance can provide attractive lighting but can also become a torture device. Chernobyl, earthquakes, AIDS and the pointless violence of Heysel stadium. The nihilist points to all these tragedies and gloom and doom descends. The artist Damian Hirst has expressed this attitude to life: 'It depresses me to think that you can pick up a phone and order a shark, but that's the way the world is. Trying to do the right thing seems so futile.'[6]

4. Solution? There is No Solution

The hippy believed that a solution to the world's problems existed. Spike the water systems with 'acid' and all will be bliss. The Nazis believed that Hitler would bring a perfect world for the chosen Aryan race. Karl Marx believed that the communist revolution would usher in a golden age. The nihilist is contemptuous of all such 'final' solutions. There is no solution. Evil and death will triumph; truth, beauty and justice are losers. At the end of the day love, peace and justice are bound to be relegated.

5 Be cynical!

Life's a bitch and then you die. This might be a nihilist slogan. No hope, no purpose, no future. There is no life after death and there is no life before death. Only drudgery, frustration and irritation. In the light of this belief, many nihilists adopt a profoundly cynical attitude to life. Their faces are easily contorted into a sneering grin. Enthusiasm, passion and sincerity must be rejected and mocked.

This cynical, sneering attitude can often lead to an emotional detachment from life. Don't get involved! It will only hurt you! This cynical detachment from life is communicated very successfully in a song by the Smiths:

Death of a Disco Dancer
The death of a disco dancer
well, it happens a lot 'round here
and if you think Peace
is a common goal,

well, that goes to show
just how little you know
The death of a disco dancer
well I'd rather not get involved
I never talk to my neighbour
I'd just rather not get involved

6. *There is no morality*

In the context of a meaningless world and a futile life, the nihilist rejects all moral notions of good and evil. If everything is pointless and if everything is to end in oblivion, what is the source of justice and morality? Johnny Rotten posed this question when he said, 'When there's no future/ How can there be sin?'[7]

The Leopold and Loeb murder case of the 1920s might help to clarify this point. These two friends had come to believe that since God did not exist, they were free to invent their own moral code. 'Superior' individuals (like themselves) were no longer bound by 'natural law' or God's law and so could treat 'inferior' individuals with complete contempt. They acted out this attitude to life by murdering an acquaintance of theirs – simply to show the world that they were no longer subject to normal, everyday morality. The ensuing court case shocked the world.

Nihilism may seem to be a very unusual and disturbing attitude to life but it is increasingly popular.

Notes

1. Quoted in Steve Turner, *Hungry for Heaven* (London: Virgin, 1988), p141.
2. *Ibid.* p73.
3. *Ibid.* p137.
4. Bertrand Russell, 'A Free Man's Worship' in *Mysticism and Logic* (George Allen & Unwin Ltd: London, 1910), p47.
5. Quoted from John Russell, *Francis Bacon* (Methuen: London, 1965), p1.

6. Quoted in *The Guardian* (July 30th, 1992).
7. *Hungry for Heaven* p140.

Jim Morrison

It was a winter's day in 1955 in the snowy Sangre de Cristo mountains of New Mexico. A twelve year old boy named Jim Morrison was out tobogganing with his family. Clambering onto the wooden toboggan with his younger brother Andy and sister Anne, Jim made sure that he was positioned at the rear. Soon they were hurtling down the slope at breakneck speed. Suddenly Andy yelled 'bail out! bail out!'.

His galoshes had been caught under the front of their toboggan. As he pushed back to free himself, so Jim pushed forward to prevent his escape. To Andy's horror a large cabin lay directly in their path. A horrific accident seemed certain until Jim's father came to their rescue.

As Anne tumbled out, she babbled about how Jim had held them in and pushed them faster down the slope. Jim just stood there and declared coolly: 'We were just having a good time'.

As Morrison grew up, he read books voraciously. He developed a particular interest in the writings of the German philosopher Friedrich Nietzsche. A crucial influence in his life was Aldous Huxley's *The Doors of Perception*. This book convinced him of the need to 'break on through to the other side' of reality. This breakthrough was to be achieved with the aid of any drug he could get his hands on. Interestingly, his newly formed rock band took its name from the title of the book. Thus 'The Doors' were born.

As the band progressed, albeit falteringly, Jim was given the opportunity to state its philosophy in a fact sheet on the group. This he did lucidly: 'I like ideas about the breaking away or overthrowing of established order – I am interested in anything about revolt, disorder, chaos, especially activity that seems to have no meaning.'

Jim was nothing if not consistent and his lifestyle was suitably chaotic. He would often bounce along Sunset Strip in Hollywood blind drunk, playing matador with fast-moving cars. During the making of one of his short films, he planned to tie a rope around his waist and dance along the ledge of a seventeen storey building. But when he got there, to the alarm of his friends, he did his little dance without any rope, even taking the time to urinate over the ledge.

In particular, Jim enjoyed his ability to manipulate crowds. During one concert in Chicago he decided to put his skills to the test. Ripping through all their most provocative songs, Jim stirred up the crowd by throwing himself on the floor, leaping and writhing in mock agony, thrusting maracas down his leather trousers and then throwing them into the audience. After two encores, the Doors left the building with the crowd baying for more. One crazy fan leapt from the balcony, hitting the ground with a thud, only to rise up and proclaim 'Wow! What a turn-on!'

The crowd went wild and the riot was only quelled by the kicking and clubbing force of a large police presence.

Morrison was addicted to vast quantities of both alcohol and drugs. This outrageous and hedonistic lifestyle was to catch up with him when he was found dead in the bath-tub of his Paris hotel room in 1971.

For further reflection

1. In what sense could we refer to Jim Morrison as a nihilist?
2. Imagine that you are Jim's girlfriend, Pamela Courson. What is it like to live with Jim?
3. Play the class the Doors song *Riders on the Storm*. Analyse the lyrics and point out the nihilist themes.

Source: J. Hopkins and D. Sugerman, *No One Here Gets Out Alive* (Plexus, 1980).

Francis Bacon

Francis Bacon was born in Dublin on October 28th 1909. He was one of five children. His father, an army veteran, earned his living as a horse-trainer.

In 1914, when war broke out, Bacon's father took a job in the War Office and the family moved to London. They moved back and forth between Ireland and England but never really settled. Bacon enjoyed a varied education and experienced far more independence than was usual for the time. He would often visit his grandmother for extended periods, revelling in the constant stream of eccentric guests that she often entertained.

One of his great aunts married a Mitchell from Newcastle, a well-to-do family, who possessed all manner of fascinating stately homes and castles. For Francis this exotic and unusual life was quite normal. Nevertheless, the art-critic, John Russell, has argued that his experience of the eccentric British gentry had a profound impact on his later life and work.

Though Bacon's father was a keen gambler, he retained a puritanical fervour with respect to sexual indiscretion. When Francis was discovered trying on some of his mother's clothing, he was sent away from the family home. He found himself completely free to go his own way and resolved that his key aim in life would be 'to do nothing'. He moved around from place to place, observing with interest the pretensions and idiosyncracies of a host of family friends.

In 1928 he spent a brief but important time in Berlin. Here, Bacon was able to fully explore his hedonistic desires; with passion and commitment he pushed every pleasurable activity to its furthest extent.

Perhaps the reason for this extreme behaviour can be traced back to his reflections on the misery and futility of life and death. When he was seventeen Bacon had concluded, 'I remember it very, very clearly. I remember looking at a dog 'muck' on the pavement and I suddenly realized, there it is – this is what life is like.'

Bacon's grim outlook on life was not to be translated into artistic endeavour for some years. In the 1930's he worked chiefly as a designer and decorator. When the second world war began, his asthmatic condition ruled him out of active service and he enrolled in the ARP Rescue Service, only to be discharged for ill-health. After this, painting began to assume a much more prominent role in his life and in April 1945, he made a dramatic impact on the artistic world.

His 'Three Studies for Figures at the Base of a Crucifixion' shocked a nation heady with victory. Completely at odds with the prevalent triumphalism, his images of awful, twisted, diabolical creatures were so unexpected that many wrote them off as freakish. Yet as time progressed and the full horror of the war came to light, they took on a startling pertinence. Bacon wanted to communicate that life was 'rotten to the core' and he declared that 'we are all carcasses'.

His debut was to set him on course for the quintessential bohemian lifestyle. He became a leading light in Soho drinking circles and was well-known for viewing London as a 'sexual gymnasium'.

His artistic output consistently illustrated his contention that whilst there was no heaven there most definitely was a hell – here on earth! As he put it so well: 'Man now realizes that he is an accident, that he is a completely futile being, that he has to play out the game without reason.'

In a series of interviews with David Sylvester in 1975, Bacon denied that he had ever set out to horrify people. His aim was simply to portray life as it was, to expose the 'naked truth'. If that was horrifying, then so be it.

For further reflection

1. What evidence is there to suggest that Bacon embraced a nihilist outlook on life?
2. Why might a nihilist adopt a very permissive lifestyle?
3. How does Bacon's artistic work reflect his nihilism?

Source: John Russell, *Francis Bacon* (Thames and Hudson: London, 1971).

Kurt Cobain

Kurt Cobain was born on 20th February 1967. His early years were spent in the small coastal town of Aberdeen in Washington state. He was a happy and gifted child but he was devastated when his mother and father decided to divorce when he was only eight years old.

Kurt spent the rest of his childhood moving from his father to his mother; at times he would stay with various uncles. This restless, brooding lifestyle was debilitating and emotionally draining; he became increasingly morose and dissatisfied with life.

He spent his years at high school, experimenting with pot and LSD, desperately trying to form a punk-rock band but none of his friends seemed sufficiently inspired to team up with him. In 1985 he persuaded the drummer of a band called the Melvins to record a demo tape of a few songs that Cobain had written. They recorded these songs on a home recorder at one of Kurt's aunt's houses; Cobain dubbed this collection 'Fecal Matter'. In 1987 after listening to the tape, a friend of Kurt's, Chris Novoselic, suggested that he and Kurt should form a band.

After numerous name changes, a succession of drummers and endless gigs, the two hopeful stars settled on the name Nirvana and teamed up with the drummer, Chad Channing. Soon they were spotted by a small but influential Seattle-based label Sub-pop and they recorded a single – Love Buzz. Only a thousand copies of the single were pressed and they quickly sold out.

In the June of 1989, the band released their debut album – 'Bleach'. This was an instant success and in 1990 the drummer Chad Channing was discarded in favour of David Grohl. A much bigger label, DGC, quickly signed them. In September 1991 they released their major label debut album, 'Nevermind'. For many this album was a masterpiece, combining crunching guitar riffs with superb melodies. The album was written completely and solely by Kurt Cobain and has sold some ten million copies throughout the world. Nirvana mania had arrived and Kurt had become a famous and wealthy rock star.

In the last three years of his life, Kurt (and his notorious wife, Courtney Love), constantly enjoyed the limelight. Cobain despised his celebrity and mocked the pretensions of the rock star. Haunted by heroin addiction and severe stomach pains, Kurt was becoming increasingly bitter and cynical. Nihilist themes infused his lyrics and on one occasion he remarked: 'For the best part of my life, my attitude has been totally negative and nihilist'. On one infamous occasion when Nirvana appeared on 'Top of the Pops', Cobain changed the first line of the song 'Smells Like Teen Spirit' to, 'Load up on drugs and kill your friends'.

Cobain's personal demons and struggles finally caught up with him. He had wanted to call his last album, *I Hate Myself And I Want To Die*! Tragically he was found dead on the 8th of April, 1994. He had blown away his head with a shotgun.

For further reflection

1. What evidence is there to suggest that Cobain embraced a nihilist outlook on life?
2. How does the optimism of the hippy movement contrast with the cynicism of a singer like Kurt Cobain?
3. What is the nihilist understanding of human nature? (See section 2 of this chapter.)

Source: *Mega Metal* Issue 2 (April 1994).

Leopold and Loeb

As a student of law at the University of Chicago in 1924, Nathan Leopold developed an interest in philosophy and was particularly intrigued by the works of the German philosopher Friedrich Nietzsche.

Nietzsche had argued that 'God is dead'. He proceeded to unravel the implications of this declaration. If there is no God, then there is no divine moral code. Men and women are free to create their own morality. Echoing Darwin's famous theory, Nietzsche reasoned that given the cruelty of evolution, strong, superior humans must assert their power and dominance. Weak and inferior people were valueless and 'ripe for destruction'. In this dramatic and bloody struggle for survival, Nietzsche believed that 'supermen' would emerge free from the fetters of traditional morality.

Nathan and his friend Richard Loeb believed that they were such 'supermen'. Without God, such exalted beings had taken God's place. The realisation of 'divine status' had a powerful impact upon Leopold and Loeb. Together they planned to exercise the unrestricted power that this implied.

The first illustration of their power came with the theft of a portable typewriter from the University of Michigan. This small act was unworthy of 'superior' beings and they decided to add swindling and murder to the list. This would be sure to alleviate their boredom.

Creating a false identity – Ballard – Leopold hired a car, which the two youths drove to a stretch of open country. There they found a group of boys playing ball and decided to wait for a potential victim. Eventually a Jewish boy named Robert Franks left the game and began to walk home. Being an acquaintance of the two young men, he gratefully accepted a lift home. He was rapidly gagged and struck on the head with a chisel; he died instantly, even though the the pair had planned to kill him later by jointly strangling him with a rope.

At dusk they drove to a marsh, stripped the body and disfigured the face with hydrochloric acid, before dumping it. They then posted a ransom letter to the victim's father, saying that he was still alive. But before any ransom could be paid, the body was discovered.

The police were perplexed by the case. An inquisitive reporter began to investigate the mysterious murder. Fortunately for him, a member of the public furnished him with a piece of vital evidence. Leopold had inadvertently left a pair of distinctive, horn-rimmed glasses at the scene of the crime. Consulting a local optician, the reporter was able to link Leopold to the glasses. This proved to be his undoing. Both men were sentenced to life imprisonment.

For further thought

1. What are some common motives for murder?
2. What motivated Leopold and Loeb to commit a murder that shocked a nation?
3. In what sense can Leopold and Loeb be described as nihilists?

Brief Notes

This murder is unusual because of its motive. Normally a murder is committed because of jealousy, greed, revenge, lust, etc. The motive for this murder is intimately connected to the atheistic beliefs of Leopold and Loeb. If God is dead, then there is no morality.

Source: Richard Glyn Jones, ed., *The Giant Book of True Crime* (Magpie Books: London, 1992).

PRIMAL RELIGIONS

INTRODUCTION

The Observer magazine carried an intriguing story about the initiation of a white South African witch doctor.

> A white woman kneels in the centre of a hardened cow-dung floor,
> surrounded by 100 or more Zulus. The Zulus wear an assortment of
> beads and animal skins, and they are dancing to an incessant drum
> beat which reverberates around the grass and mud hut. The woman
> is about 30 years old, and is looking nervously at a white goat held
> upright in front of her by a couple of black youths. They spread open
> its legs as a razor-sharp short spear, an *assegai*, is pressed against
> the animal's belly. The goat lets out a terrified scream. A murmur of
> approval goes up from the spectators.
>
> The assegai is plunged into the beast's heart, killing it swiftly. The
> woman bends down and puts her lips to the wound; the blood trickles
> down her chin. During the week this woman works as a state prosecutor
> in the country's courts. Today, in this remote *kraal* in the rolling hills of
> Zululand, she has just completed her initiation as a witch doctor.[1]

We might well ask why a white woman has chosen to become
a witch doctor? Why was this woman willing to take part in this
bloody and violent ceremony? What exactly are witch doctors?
To answer these questions we will need to understand 'primal'
religions.

Key Beliefs of Primal Religions

1. Primal? Tribal? Animist?

Various terms have been used to designate the type of religion that we encounter in this Zulu initiation ceremony: 'animist', 'atavist', 'tribal' and 'primitive', among others. The choice of term is controversial, and it is hard to find a word which will please everyone.

The most recent trend in the study of religion is to refer to this type of religion as 'primal'. Primal religions are those religions that predate the great historic religions of Judaism, Christianity, Islam, Hinduism and Buddhism. They are sometimes referred to as 'polytheistic' religions and include the ancient pagan religions that we studied in our chapter on 'pagan' religion. The focus in this chapter will be upon African primal religions.

Before the growth of the major world religions, the primal religions appeared to influence all human societies. Different groups or tribes seemed to possess their own particular religious perspectives. It is important to appreciate that there are many different 'primal' religions but there would seem to be a common core; it is possible to distil common themes and assumptions.

2. The Supreme Creator is Distant

In many primal religions there is a belief in a Supreme Creator but this Creator is portrayed as distant and unconcerned with human affairs. This Creator has withdrawn from his creation. In some sense human beings have offended this 'most high' God and in anger he has left the earth and retreated to heaven. This primal concept of a distant God can be found in the religion of the Nigerian Tiv tribe.

> In the beginning Aondo dwelt near the earth and personally watched over it. One day, however, as a woman was preparing food by pounding yams in her mortar, she struck her pestle against Aondo,

and he in hurt anger left the earth and now dwells in the heavens. Indeed, the word for sky is Aondo, and the clouds are his spots.[2]

Aondo is perceived by the Tiv people as a disgruntled, rather grumpy deity who dwells in lonely exile. This belief contributes to a profound fatalism among the Tiv people; an earthquake might occur and the Tiv people will shrug their shoulders and declare, 'It's only Aondo.'

Aondo's absence from the earth means that inferior spiritual beings are in complete control of earthly life. These spirits are believed to be fickle, capricious 'nature' spirits who dwell in trees, mountains and rivers. David Burnett comments as follows:

> Nature is influenced by these various spiritual beings and forces which are capricious and able to disturb the balance of nature. Humans must therefore ally themselves with the forces of good which cause the annual cycle of nature to bring forth its harvest. Failure to do so would disturb the balance and bring disaster upon the whole tribe. Human beings exist in a complex and dangerous world of seen and unseen powers and beings.[3]

These invisible 'supernatural' powers must be respected and obeyed. Upset them and there will be trouble. Primal religions are preoccupied with the correct response to these unseen beings.

3. Shamans and Sorcerers

An unusual feature of primal religion is the belief in the 'external soul'. A soul, it is believed, can leave the confines of a person's body without the person dying. A sorcerer or a witch can 'steal' a person's soul and the individual will become lethargic, sickly and may even die. A witch can leave her body and enter the body of a lion. In the form of the lion, the witch may well kill and devour her enemy. This belief in the 'external soul' leads to a belief in bilocation; a person can be lying in bed asleep and yet perform a murder ten miles away!

Diagnosis of sickness and illness is greatly influenced by the belief in the 'external soul'. The witch doctor or shaman is perceived as a good person who is primarily concerned with the well-being of the tribe. The shaman uses drugs, charms, sacrifices, chantings and dancing rituals; with great skill this person gains entry to the spirit world and is then able to restore harmony between the spirit world and the human world.

If a person's soul has been stolen by a witch or a sorcerer, the witch doctor will 'find' the lost soul and then he will return it to the sickly, lethargic victim. If an illness has been caused by a malevolent spirit the shaman will evict the mischievous spirit with the use of magic.

4 Magic

Various kinds of magic are used. Sympathetic or imitative magic focuses on the belief that like produces like. A rain dance might well involve the spewing of water into the air to make rain fall. A poisoned arrow might be plunged into the footprint of an enemy.

In contagious magic the part stands for the whole; what is done to a part affects the whole from which it comes. This is why a sorcerer can make harmful charms from a man's waste hair, nails, clothing and from the placenta and naval cord of babies. These articles are often hidden very carefully lest a witch should find them and use them to harmful effect.

In an African primal context 'white' magic is understood as a protective, healing use of supernatural power. White magic is practised by medicine men, diviners, rainmakers and witch doctors. 'Black' magic is a power which uses supernatural forces for evil ends. Black magicians, sorcerers or wizards are feared and hated. The belief in their existence might explain the popularity of witch doctors in Soweto.

5. Belief in Ancestral Spirits

In many primal societies it is believed that ancestral spirits have considerable impact upon the affairs of men and women. The spirits of the ancestors are supposed to live beneath the surface of the earth where their bodies have been buried. These ancestors are believed to be the real owners of the land and cattle. The present living people have received the land from their ancestors and they are duty-bound to care for and use it so the present generations might be continued. They are responsible to the ancestors for preserving the land and cattle for future generations. These departed spirits do not lose interest in their property. If family herds are squandered then the ancestral spirits will punish the offending parties.

These ancestors are ever at hand to help or to harm. If an ancestor has been improperly buried or offended when alive, it is often believed that he might seek revenge by bringing some misfortune to the living heir. The character of an ancestral spirit is often believed to reflect to some extent the character of the person from whom it came. A bitter person would become a bitter, brooding spirit! More importantly, the power of the spirit is intimately connected with the position he formerly had held in the tribe. Faithful communion with ancestral spirits ensures a good relationship and avoids disturbances which might be caused if they are neglected.

A shaman is the tribe's troubleshooter. A problem such as a failed harvest might be caused by sorcery; it might be caused by unhappy ancestors. The sacrifice of a goat might be appropriate appeasement for a distressed and grieving dead grandmother.

6. Community

Western people may be surprised at the depth of commitment that an African can show to his family and his tribe. Western consumerists are supreme individualists who are primarily concerned with *their* accumulation of wealth. Their desire to maximise their wealth is the driving force of their lives. The primal attitude encourages respect and devotion to the wider social unit be it the family or the tribe. Important decisions are made by the community. A young woman, for example, will be willing to marry a man of her father's choosing because it is good for the family.

7. Fragile

Primal worldviews are basically fragile and can easily fracture on contact with larger societies. The primal attitude distrusts science and sophisticated technology; ancestor worship activates a great fear of change and innovation. There are many stories of primal peoples who reject western technology for the simple reason that the ancestral spirits do not like change. At the same time there can be a dangerous fascination with all things western. Nambiquara Indians of the Amazon forest are both repelled and fascinated by guns, aeroplanes and cans of diet coke.

This distrust of and flirtation with western consumerism can lead to the tragic demise of many so-called primitive tribes. The Nambiquara is a good example. This unfortunate tribe was first contacted by Europeans in 1911; since then they have been ravaged by the white man's illnesses, flu and measles. By 1945 nineteen out of every twenty of the population had died. This has had a devastating impact upon the Nambiquara way of life. David Burnett comments:

> Families were torn apart, children orphaned, wives were widowed. One village now contains the survivors of forty-three villages. The world had come to an end! Women no longer wanted to have children because they saw no point in them being born into a world they saw as falling apart. They were a depressed people, a weakened people, a people who needed time to recover. . . The Nambiquara are a dispirited people who attribute the epidemic to white man's black magic.[4]

In Brazil it is common to see native people who have been 'corrupted' by the western way of life. People who once lived in dark forests, sip their pepsis and smoke their Marlboros. Primal religions are very easily disrupted by the western way of life.

And all this brings us back to our white witch doctor. She underwent this rather bloody initiation ceremony because she had come to believe in the efficacy of white magic. This woman had become a troubleshooter for those who feared both witches and ancestral spirits.

Notes

1. *Observer* Magazine, 29th August 1993.
2. Eugene Rubingh, *Sons of Tiv* (Baker Book House: Grand Rapids, 1969), pp71-72.
3. David Burnett, *Clash of Worlds* (Monarch: Eastbourne, 1990), p59.
4. *Ibid.* p127.

Witchdoctors

Read the story about the white woman witch doctor at the beginning of this chapter.

For further thought

1. It is estimated that in the township of Soweto, there are some 8,000 practising witch doctors. Why do you think that this is such a popular 'career option'?
2. Why might a typical consumerist abandon their traditional beliefs and become a witch doctor?
3. What kinds of magic would a witchdoctor employ? (See section 4 of this chapter.)

Schakipera and Kimbiri

The famous anthropologist Lucien Levy Bruhl records this intriguing story about two Azande natives.

Two neighbours, Schakipera and Kimbiri, go to the wood to gather honey. Possibly Schakipera was the more adroit, or it may have been mere luck, but at any rate he found four big trees full of honey whilst Kimbiri could only find one. When he reached home again, Kimbiri was bewailing the fact that he had had such bad luck, while his neighbour had been so fortunate. Meanwhile Schakipera has returned to the wood at once with his relatives in order to bring away the honey he had found. In the evening he was attacked and torn in pieces by a lion. His companions hastily climbed trees and thus saved themselves.

His affrighted relatives at once go to the *kimbanda* (soothsayer) to discover who was really responsible for his death. The *kimbanda* consults the oracle several times and finally declares that Kimbiri, jealous of his neighbour's rich harvest of honey, assumed the form of a lion in order to avenge himself. . . The soothsayer's judgement was reported to the ruler of Kiakka, and he, in the face of the accused's strenuous denial, ordered the matter to be settled by the ordeal of poison. . . The ordeal was unfavourable to the accused, he confesses, and succumbs to torture.[1]

For further thought

1. How would the concept of the 'external soul' help us to understand this story?
2. How would a nihilist interpretation of the death of Schakipera differ from that of the *Kimbanda* (soothsayer)?

3. The ruler of Kiakka has accused you of sorcery. You must undergo an ordeal of poison. What might you write in your diary for that day?

Brief Notes

A nihilist would say that the death of Schakipera was a meaningless event in a purposeless universe. The Azande, on the other hand, would point to the possibility of a sorcerer taking possession of the lion and using it as an instrument of murder. Bilocation is a possible explanation for the Azande; it is certainly not for the nihilist.

Source: Lucien Levy Bruhl, *The Soul of the Primitive* (George Allen and Unwin: London, 1965), p44.

Blood-feuding

Squeezed between Serbia, Montenegro and Macedonia in the North and Greece in the South, lies the small nation of Albania. Its population of about 3 million is less than half that of London.

Albania came into existence in 1913 when the Ottoman empire collapsed. Even so, its people – The Illyrians – are the most ancient of European races.

In the modern world, Albania is most clearly associated with a Stalinist-style communism. From 1945 until 1985 the megalomaniacal leader Enver Hoxha dominated this obscure European nation. In 1967 he declared Albania the 'first atheist republic in the world', issuing a ban on all acts of public worship and executing anyone who dared to disobey.

However in his attempts to transform Albanian society into a Stalinist utopia, Hoxha found himself up against the deep-seated and little known practice of blood-feuding. This practice requires what Albanians call 'gjak per gjak' or blood for blood. It is enshrined in the 'Kanun', a primitive constitution transmitted by word of mouth down the generations. The laws of the Kanun regulate the arrangement of marriages, the boundaries of fields and the payment of taxes. Failure to observe these statutes can lead to severe penalties; these include death and the burning of a man's harvest.

Any quarrel, no matter how insignificant, can involve a loss of family honour. An offense to a man's honour can often lead to a bitter and long-lasting blood feud. The killing of a sheep-dog, even a dispute over a game of cards can lead to a person's death.

Selimaj, an old man from the town of Valbona, tells the story of a feud between two families that erupted after the theft of shotgun cartridges; 30 lives were lost over three generations before the argument was settled.

No surprise then that Hoxha's collective farms proved unpopular. As one Albanian farmer puts it:-

> Hoxha promised a paradise of collective farms. If we refused to surrender we'd have been branded as kulaks (land-owning peasants liquidated by Stalin for opposing collectivisation) and shot on the spot. Now I want it back. Every last hectare of my stolen land. Blood calls for blood.

Indeed a significant number of Albanians wish to see the return of the monarchy in the shape of King Leka, now exiled in South Africa. Leka claims that the communists 'imposed a foreign ideology which had nothing to do with Albanian culture! Communism never allowed for honour or mercy in the way that the tribes certainly did.'

Hoxha also faced great difficulties when he tried to raise the status of women. The Kanun code states that 'a wife is a sack for carrying things', and Albanian men were not about to relinquish this tradition. Indeed it is the custom during a wedding for the bride's parents to give the groom a 'trousseau bullet' with which he has the right to kill his wife should she try to leave him. This custom was banned under communism but many Albanians still approve of it.

In contrast to this the Kanun also stresses the importance of looking after guests. Hospitality to guests is considered so important that a household is bound to exact reparation for any injury done to a guest as though they were a member of the family.

It seems that despite the promises of the newly democratically elected government many Albanians see a return to the Kanun as the answer to their problems. As one Albanian, Fran Lleshi, puts it, 'You'll see! The Kanun will bring my country to the eve of a great deliverance.'

For further thought

1. What is the Kanun? How does the Kanun clash with communist principles?
2. What is blood-feuding?
3. What is 'family honour'? How is the Mafia influenced by this impulse?

Brief Notes

The Kanun, like the Mosaic law, is a deeply religious document. 'Family honour' is of sacred significance to the Illyrian people. In a sense the 'family' has become an object of worship. In primal religions the family or tribe is highly honoured.

This contrasts strikingly with the central importance of the state in Stalinist communism.

Source: *Observer* Magazine (21st July 1992).

Setyo's Story

Setyo was walking along one day when his dead grandmother 'spoke' to him. She said to Setyo (faithful) 'Come and join me.' Setyo was confused. 'How can I join you?' he said to this 'voice'. His 'grandmother' told him to go home, pour paraffin all over his body and to light a match.

That was the way for Setyo to 'join' his grandmother. Setyo did as the voice commanded; he did not die instantly but died a horrible death in hospital. As he lay dying a missionary from England prayed for him with a friend. As Setyo lay dying he kept shouting, 'Mount Kawi is a place of fire.'

The missionary and his friend went to the home of Setyo's mother. They told her of Setyo's agonising death. The mother was cold and unmoved. In Java, Mount Kawi is an infamous place, a place of death. Here it is that the people bargain with the spirits.

Michael and his friend questioned the woman. Why did she seem so unperturbed, so unresponsive? Her boy had just died in the most painful way. It transpired that, the day before, she had bargained with the spirits on Mount Kawi. She had offered her son as a sacrifice. In Java it is believed that if you make a bargain with the spirits and they accept it, they will bless you. She had traded her son for a prosperous future. The spirits had accepted her sacrifice.

For further thought

1. What might motivate a person to 'bargain' with the spirits?
2. What aspect of primal religion might induce a person like

Setyo to obey his grandmother?
3. Devise a dialogue between Michael, his friend and Setyo's mother.

Brief Notes

This macabre story illustrates the respect given to dead ancestors in some primal contexts. The technical term for this is 'atavism'.

Source: This story comes from a missionary who spent many years in Indonesia.

CHRISTIANITY

INTRODUCTION

An ex-president of the USA Jimmy Carter clutches a nail in his left hand and picks up a hammer. He is working with a team of volunteers renovating New York tenements for low-income families.

Since leaving office in 1979, Carter has continued to be involved in the 'big world of politics'. He has spent a great deal of time negotiating with some of the key leaders of Africa to end bloody and violent wars; he has sponsored and inspired numerous humanitarian programmes. These include agricultural projects in Ghana and a campaign to eradicate the 'Guinea' worm; a parasite that afflicts some 10 million Africans. Jimmy Carter is passionate about such issues.

Carter's impressive influence in world affairs is such that *Time* magazine rates him as one of the best ex-presidents of the USA.! And yet this same 'important' man is committed to a Christian missionary organisation known as Habitat for Humanity.

Habitat for Humanity is a movement initiated by a Georgian neighbour of Carter's, one Millard Fuller. Fuller is committed to the construction of houses for poor people who are not able to buy houses of their own. Habitat for Humanity is involved in housing projects in over 450 communities across the United States and around the world.

Each day some six houses are finished and sold to poor families at only the cost of construction. No deposit is required and no interest is included in the cost of the mortgage. Fuller's organisation does not charge interest because of Fuller's reading of the Bible. The Mosaic law is most emphatic that when lending to the poor, interest must not be charged: 'If you lend money to one of my people among you who is needy, do not be like a money-lender; charge him no interest' (Exodus 22:25).

Fuller's interpretation of this Mosaic teaching is provocative. He argues that it is permissible to charge interest when lending money to the rich but this is inappropriate when it comes to the poor. When the poor borrow money it is usually because of desperate circumstances and the Mosaic law requires that such people should not be exploited by those who have the means to help them. This biblical principle is a key feature of Habitat for Humanity.

And so Jimmy Carter will sometimes help out as a volunteer in the construction of these homes for the poor. Both Fuller and Carter have been inspired by the teaching of the Bible.

What would prompt a very influential and 'important' man to become a labourer in such an organisation? Why would a millionaire and an ex-president of the USA pick up the blunt end of a shovel? To answer this intriguing question we will need to examine the key Christian beliefs of men like Fuller and Carter.

Key Beliefs of Christianity

Christians do not always agree with each other. There are many different interpretations of the biblical revelation. We can speak of fundamentalist, liberal, scholastic and redemptive-historical ways of reading and understanding the Bible. And even this brief list is too cursory and simplified. It is not an easy task to summarise Christian belief and practice! (Exactly the same point could be made in our accounts of Hinduism, Islam, consumerism etc.)

But an attempt must be made. The following interpretation of the biblical revelation is sometimes referred to as a redemptive-historical approach. The redemptive-historical way of reading and understanding the Bible emphasises three key biblical themes – creation, fall and redemption. Some Christians would find this approach unacceptable but we believe that this interpretation is a faithful reading of the biblical material.

1. Creation

The gnostic tends to believe that the world is an evil place. There are Hindus who believe that the world is an illusion. For many consumerists the world is viewed as a stockpile of raw materials. The Bible does not articulate any of these views.

The first chapter of the book of Genesis states emphatically that the world that God has made is good. God made the sea and God saw that it was good. God made the stars, the planets and the sun and God saw that they were good. God made the ferret, the hamster and the gerbil and God saw that they were good. God made the tulip, the buttercup and the bluebell and God saw that they were good.

This repeated refrain sets the scene for the biblical way of understanding. Again and again we are reminded of the glory and beauty of God's good creation.

When a teacher marks a young student's homework, she can learn so much about her student from that work. Is the student conscientious? Does she understand the lesson? Is she able to develop her own ideas? A good teacher can learn a great deal about little Tracy from that essay. Perhaps Tracy is slothful, careless and linguistically challenged. The teacher will soon find out by 'considering the works of her hand'.

In just the same way, the biblical revelation tells us what human beings can learn about God from the creation. Psalm 19 tells us that:

The heavens declare the glory of God;
the skies proclaim the work of his hands.
Day after day they pour fourth speech;
night after night they display knowledge.

Psalm 19:1–2

It is easy to see that Tracy has injected something of herself into her writing. In just the same way Christians believe that God has infused the world with his colourful personality. The creation is rich, colourful and interesting because God is rich, colourful and interesting.

But to whom does this colourful world belong? The Nazi might well retort – The Aryan race! An animist from Madagascar might beg to differ, and talk about his ancestors. Psalm 24 presents an entirely different response.

The earth is the Lord's, and everything in it,
the world, and all who live in it;
for he founded it upon the seas
and established it upon the waters.

Psalm 24:1–2

According to the biblical revelation, the world is a good and immensely valuable piece of property and this piece of real estate belongs to God.

It is also important to appreciate the biblical contention that the world display's God's wisdom. The planet earth offers ideal opportunities for the harmonious growth of plants, shrubs, bushes and trees. Water, air, soil and abundant minerals create the perfect setting for human life. Unlike Uranus, earth teems with the optimum temperatures and appropriate fluid levels. Too much water would be a nightmare; too little a catastrophe – this particular property has a great deal going for it!

2. The Cultural Mandate

The Orphic myth had suggested that heaven was man's true home. Orphism activated a profound sense of exile in the human heart; earth is a painful and deeply unfulfilling location. The Orphic and the gnostic longed to escape from this earthly prison.

The Bible presents an entirely different perspective. God created men and women and placed them on the earth for a specific purpose. He gave them a task. . . . .a purpose. . . . .a raison d'etre. . . . .a commission.

> God blessed them and said to them, 'Be fruitful and increase in number; fill the earth and subdue it. Rule over the fish of the sea and the birds of the air and over every living creature that moves on the ground.'
>
> Gen 1:28

Humans are creatures who exercise enormous power. We build huge bridges; we construct skyscrapers and helicopters. Men tunnel through the hardest rock in search of hidden treasures. With impressive ingenuity, humans fashion necklaces, crowns and tiaras. All this takes power; an ability to rule, direct and unfold.

The earth invites us, beckons us to explore and unfold. Humans discover oil and in time they have developed plastic. A tree becomes a chair. A piece of marble can become a stunning statue. A waterfall can be translated into electrical power. Iron ore can be banged, whacked and attacked and magically becomes a knife to peel an apple. Words can become poems. Musical notes bring forth elaborate and sophisticated symphonies. Such is the power of humankind.

The Bible teaches that this power is given to us by God. And in using this power we are like God. We resemble God by ruling, unfolding and developing. The world is filled with treasures and surprises waiting to be unveiled, discovered and perfected.

But this is only half the story. In Genesis chapter 2 we discover something new: 'The Lord God took the man and put him in the Garden of Eden to work it and take care of it' (Genesis 2:15).

As humans unfold the rich potentials of the earth, they are also commanded by God to look after the world. The unfolding of music, drama, comedy, cities, commerce and agriculture must not lead to the earth's destruction. Careful preservation of the garden is as much an imperative as the command to unfold. Cities can be built without ecological damage. Culture can be unfolded without human misery and oppression.

This then is what we mean by the cultural mandate – humans are called to rule and to serve the world that God has created. Just as God has shaped and moulded the earth into a brilliant work of art, so we must follow in God's footsteps. But powerful and creative humans must rule with wisdom and justice.

3. The Fall

Why then is there so much evil and destruction in this good creation? How does the biblical revelation account for the presence of death, war, injustice and cruelty? The Orphic tradition accounted for evil in terms of a fall from heaven; the earth and the body is the source and origin of all evil. The Scripture presents an entirely different account.

The Old Testament teaches that early in human history, human beings rebelled against God and became ensnared by evil, deceiving powers. The covenant or treaty between God and humankind was broken and a curse began to consume the earth (Isaiah 24:1–13). The exact nature of this curse becomes clear when we investigate it systematically.

(i) God's relationship to humans has become damaged and distorted. God has withdrawn from a sinful world. Humans, from their side, often experience God as distant and unconcerned. Communication with God becomes a struggle and many humans can often feel abandoned by God. Conflict and fear have intruded into this relationship.

(ii) The relationship between humans is often consumed with jealousy, hatred and cruelty. There is conflict between races and nations. We live in a world filled with war and human rights abuses. There is bullying in the playground and football hooliganism.

(iii) The relationship between men and women can be fraught with pain and anxiety. There is rape and sexual harrassment; wife-battering and adultery. Men can often dominate women and women, in their turn, can become subservient, passive and manipulative. Prostitution is another part of this broken relationship. Men can often perceive women as objects to be used and abused. All this is part of the 'fall'.

(iv) The fall has also affected our relationship to ourselves. Chris can become frustrated with himself as he misses an easy goal; he swears and hurls abuse at himself. A writer struggles to finish a sentence; she clenches her fists and bites her nails. Suicide is the most extreme response to this aspect of the fall. Anorexia and bulimia are intimately connected to a distorted self-image; numerous neuroses affect the human race. This too is part of the fall.

(v) The relationship between humans and animals is corrupted and spoiled. Crocodiles can be hunted out of existence; avaricious humans can destroy elephants and rhinos; numerous species no longer exist. At the same time tigers, lions and panthers take their revenge. Conflict and fear has infused the relationship between animals and humans.

(vi) The relationship between humans and the earth is filled with violence. We pollute our seas and lakes with industrial waste; acid rain attacks forests and the ozone layer is under threat. At the same time the earth does not remain passive; volcanoes, earthquakes and hurricanes conspire against the human race with deadly venom.

Biblical teaching emphasises that this curse has ravaged the good creation; the world groans and moans with pain. Cities like Sarajevo lie desolate. Families are torn apart; widows mourn the loss of their husbands. A good friendship can disintegrate into a bitter, brooding feud. Marriages crumble.

The Bible teaches that the fall has also introduced idolatry into our lives. Instead of loving and trusting our creator we turn and worship good created things. For some money can become a false god. For others family honour can become a sacred cow. And there are those who bow down and worship economic growth or even the sun. This is the tragedy of living in a broken, fallen world.

4. Redemption, Part One

But God could not stand idly by. The pain and desperation of the human race moved the Lord God to tears of grief (Genesis 6:6). The Bible teaches that God longed to heal and rescue his broken and corrupted world. This passionate, loving God would begin a divine project of rescue. He would raise up a holy people, a godly people and through this people God would bring salvation to the world.

This process of rescue, of redemption began with a man called Abraham. God spoke to this man and made him an outrageous promise.

I will make you into a great nation
and I will bless you;
I will make your name great,
and you will be a blessing.
I will bless those who bless you,
and whoever curses you I will curse;
and all peoples on earth
will be blessed through you.

Genesis 12:2–3

Abraham had a son, named Isacc. Isacc had a son named Jacob. Jacob had twelve sons who became in time the founders of the nation of Israel.

Through Moses, God gave his law or *torah* to this people. This law showed the descendants of Abraham how to live. This law covers and includes ever conceivable issue and scenario. The holy nation must care for and preserve the land (Leviticus 25). Justice must pervade the entire life of the nation; poverty, destitution and begging were to be avoided at all costs (Deuteronomy 15). Land was to be distributed justly and fairly; orphans, widows and strangers were to be cared for. The law commanded the people to set each other free from such miseries as slavery, prostitution, debt-bondage and homelessness. The law prompted Abraham's descendants to rest, work and play in a truly original way.

The Mosaic law is full of redemptive hope and promise. Even the animals would partake of this healing word; oxen and donkeys should be treated with kindness. The purpose of the Mosaic law was to *eliminate* poverty, cruelty, injustice, misery and environmental damage from the land. God's purpose was to lift the curse that had entered the world because of 'man's first disobedience'. The Mosaic law is a redemptive law; a law that is infused with God's redemptive wisdom.

5. Redemption, Part Two

Unfortunately the Hebrew people did not obey the laws and statutes of the Mosaic law. Again and again they broke the treaty with God and turned to the worship of fertility gods such as Baal and Asherah. God sent his prophets to speak to the people and to remind them of the covenant but this divine initiative was continually frustrated and thwarted.

It was to Isaiah, the prophet, that God revealed his deepest redemptive purposes. According to the Bible, Yahweh promised to send a saviour, not just to the nation of Israel but to the whole world (Isaiah 49:6). This Messiah (Anointed One) would be both a servant and a king. He would die for the sins of the world and he would also establish peace and justice throughout the world. The Messiah would lift the curse, restore the broken covenant, proclaim the rule of God and open up the possibility of forgiveness to all peoples of the world.

Christians believe that Jesus Christ is indeed this anointed saviour. In his ministry he healed the sick, drove out evil spirits, fed hungry people and proclaimed the rule or kingdom of God. In the person of Jesus Christ, God has reasserted his right and desire to rule and reign.

And yet the life of Jesus ended in death, not in a glorious victory. To make sense of this seeming failure, we need to consider the teaching of Christ himself. He spoke very clearly of his own death and resurrection. He knew that he would die a bloody death on the cross and by this atoning death, he would restore the covenant and open up the possibility of forgiveness. But death is only the beginning and after three days the New Testament teaches that Christ returned from the grave, victorious over death. The resurrection of Jesus is the first fruit of God's victory over sin and death. It is the pledge of total redemption.

Redemption, Part Three

There are stages to this divine project of redemption. In his first coming some two thousand years ago, the Messiah laid the foundations for total redemption by his death and resurrection. But there is still more to come. Jesus Christ promised that he would come again, a second time, as a great and mighty King to judge the world and to destroy sin, death and evil completely. This last great act of redemption is still to come.

Christians believe that we are still waiting for this second coming with bated breath. The same Jesus who died on the cross will come back to the world and completely heal the world of all the ravages of sin and the curse.

The book of Revelation tells us about this new world that is coming.

> Then I saw a new heaven and a new earth, for the first heaven and the first earth had passed away, and there was no longer any sea. I

saw the New Jerusalem, coming down out of heaven from God, pre-pared as a bride beautifully dressed for her husband. And I heard a loud voice from the throne saying 'Now the dwelling of God is with men, and he will live with them. They will be his people, and God himself will be with them and be their God. He will wipe every tear from their eyes. There will be no more death or mourning or crying or pain, for the old order of things has passed away.'

Revelation 21:1–4

This then is the final goal of redemption – a new heaven and a new earth, the home of righteousness. This age to come will not be an ethereal, ghostly realm of angels and harps beyond the realms of time. This is a gnostic and not a biblical understanding of the future. Heaven will be a transformed and purified world.

Jimmy Carter and Millard Fuller are two people who have been inspired by this Christian hope. Their redemptive projects and programmes anticipate the final consummation of redemption. Christians believe that such people are living in the light of Christ's victory over sin and death.[1]

Notes

1. The story about Jimmy Carter and Millard Fuller comes from *Wake Up America* by Tony Campolo (Harper Collins Publishers: New York, 1991).

Bob Lavelle

It was once said by Harry S. Truman that banks are institutions that lend money to people who can prove that they don't need it. It was this prevailing attitude that led a young African-American Christian named Bob Lavelle to set up a bank that modelled an entirely different approach.

In the 1950's in Pittsburgh, Pennsylvania, Lavelle founded the Dwellings House Savings and Loan Association. He established this innovative project in one of the most economically disadvantaged areas of the city. His aim was to serve those that were most in need of financial backing.

This unusual bank offered loans at the lowest possible rate of interest to those people considered far too risky by other, more orthodox, banks. Lavelle's approach proved so successful that his association radically altered housing patterns in Pittsburgh and beyond. A brochure explains the logic behind this seemingly suicidal form of banking:

> Dwelling House attempts to reverse the traditional banking rule – by lending to people who may not be 'good risks', at the lowest practical interest rate. Our goal is to approach people with respect and through encouragement and patient financial counselling, to help them become good risks. This follows God's command to serve the poor and the needy.

To make this possible, the bank has a small advertising budget, modest salaries, no needless facilities, and passbook rates of 5.5%. Yet economist Bob Wauzzinski comments that:

Such sacrifices are hardly to be compared with the holistic richness gained by all who are associated with Dwelling House. Its uniqueness is manifest in its lack of an overriding notion of self-interest and state ownership and its positive influence on the economy and politics.

Since its inception the Dwelling House Savings and Loan Association has seen its working capital multiply over fourteenfold and has raised the eyebrows and sometimes the hackles of many other banks, bemused by its operating methods.

For further thought

1. What is the biblical teaching on lending money? Study Deuteronomy 15 and Exodus 22:25.
2. Devise a brochure for Dwelling House. Explain clearly the bank's Christian approach to lending money.
3. Select a bank of your choice and study its promotional literature. How does this approach to the lending of money contrast with Dwelling House?

Brief Notes

Debt Counsellor, Sheree Smith, of the Birmingham Settlement Money Advice Centre, said some of the clients who came to her for advice had been paying annual rates of repayment of between 800 and 1,000 per cent (in other words, repaying the sum borrowed every six to eight weeks in interest).

Source: Tony Campolo, *Wake Up America* (HarperCollins: New York, 1991).

Cherokees

In his book *Who Switched the Price Tags?* Tony Campolo relates a moving event that occurred at an American Baptist Convention he was chairing.

One day, as he was conducting proceedings, a group of native Americans burst in and took over. They condemned white people for their racism and then moved on to level accusations against the church. At that point a lone voice rose up in protest. It was a young Cherokee woman. She stood and made her way to the platform.

She then told the story of the 'Trail of Tears'. Years ago the Cherokees were forced to march from their homeland in Georgia to the barren lands of Oklahoma. President Andrew Jackson had called for the removal of the Cherokees from their ancient tribal lands to make way for 'white' economic interests. The young woman pointed out that only a handful of whites had stood up to the President.

> It was the missionaries who took our case before the Supreme Court. It was the missionaries, who, when they were unable to stop what the government willed for the Cherokees, took their stand with them and walked the long walk halfway across the continent.

The Cherokee woman explained that thousands of Cherokees had died on that enforced walk. Among the dead were Baptist missionaries who had chosen to identify with their oppressed friends. The story did not end there. She added:

> After the Cherokees arrived in Oklahoma, they chose some of their

strongest braves and sent them back to Georgia to dismantle the little chapel where their missionaries had once worshipped. The braves were instructed to carry the pieces of the chapel back to their new home in Oklahoma where they could be assembled for the worship of God.

When she had finished talking, a hushed silence filled the auditorium. The only sound that could be heard was the weeping of the native Americans at her side.

For further thought

1. Why were the Cherokees driven off their land?
2. Why did the Baptist missionaries accompany the Cherokees on their great trek?
3. How do native Americans like the Cherokees relate to their land? How would this contrast with the 'white man'?

Source: Tony Campolo, *Who Switched the Price Tags*? (Word: Dallas, 1986).

Deliverance Tabernacle

North Philadelphia, USA, is the kind of city zone that is studiously avoided by street-wise tourists. Drug-dealing is the principal industry, encouraging an unhealthy sideline in violent crime. The housing is barely fit for rats and children play on vacant lots covered with rubbish and abandoned cars. Unemployment is estimated at around 40% with shops closing down every day because they have been robbed too often. Even the police who patrol the area are filled with fear.

Yet, in the midst of this urban hell, something amazing is happening. A Pentecostal church is experiencing rapid growth. Incredibly, the church is committed to rebuilding the community. The ecstatic Sunday morning worship services are the launching pad for a fast expanding list of social programmes. The aim of these programmes is to redevelop the living conditions and economy of the neighbourhood.

The church, known as Deliverance Tabernacle, has organised and trained young people to repair old houses, which provides both work and good quality affordable housing. It has developed a 'total care' program for the elderly; encompassing housing, feeding and caring for many elderly people previously living in chronic loneliness.

Perhaps most striking of all is the new shopping centre they have established. This contains a supermarket, a bank and a variety of small stores. This provides employment for the local people and a safe place to shop.

The work of Deliverance Tabernacle has had such an impact in North Philadelphia that experts on urban renewal are now flying in from all over America to learn from them.

For further thought

1. Find out as much as you can about the problems that beset inner city areas in the UK.
2. What do you think has motivated the members of Deliverance Tabernacle to engage in their many and varied projects? How does this activity relate to the biblical theme of the cultural mandate?
3. You have been appointed head of 'urban renewal' in a large British city. What projects would you like to initiate?

Source: Tony Campolo, *Wake Up America* (HarperCollins: New York, 1991).

Jaime Jaramillo

Colombia is a country famous for such things as coffee, oil and cocaine. Yet scratch the surface a little and you're likely to come across a human tragedy of one kind or another. One sad example would be the street children of Bogota. Under threat from death squads, these children now reside in the only safe haven available to them, the sewers. Drowning, disease and premature death are their daily fare.

Despite this desperate situation one unlikely ray of hope exists for these children. Jaime Jaramillo is a prosperous oil exploration consultant, whose company has contracts with the likes of Exxon and Chevron. A life of luxury is his for the taking but instead he has opted to devote every spare minute to helping these beleaguered children. An incident in 1973, just before Christmas, was instrumental in turning his attention to their plight.

Walking home one day, he saw a child throw a toy box from a passing car. Two street kids dived for it and a little girl won the race. She stood there smiling and Jaime smiled back. Neither of them had seen the truck. As it hit her she was thrown into the air, and as it braked, the truck swung round and hit her again. The box was undamaged. It was also empty. She had died for nothing.

Jaime went home, disturbed and angry. He bought a Father Christmas suit and 200 toys and went round handing them out. As he handed out the toys he felt a coldness in his heart, but he persisted. Each day he found himself encountering handicapped and sick children. Whenever necessary, he would pay for hospital treatment. Before long he had 300 children in five houses and he had found work for 94 former street kids. Encouraged by his success he established a foundation – Children of the Andes.

The work in the sewers only began when a street kid pointed out to Jaime that many of her peers were now living there. Putting on breathing equipment he ventured below and began to find and rescue numerous children. Some of them were teenage mothers with new-born babies. Jaime describes the sewers with horrifying clarity:

> You have to be very strong, physically and mentally. The smell is terrible, there are rats splashing all the time, mosquitoes and leeches and flying insects. You lose your strength because it's so slippery. You have to be careful not to fall, because you get that stuff in your mouth and you have diarrhoea for 30 days.

Sadly some of the children are unaware of the many hazards that can afflict them: 'You see this froth. When it's flowing fast you get white froth and they think that the water is clean. So they wash in it and then they get terrible infections, like gangrene.'

Tragically the children also face victimisation from vigilante gangs and death squads. Indeed, many Bogotans are offended by their existence and see them as vermin to be exterminated.

Fortunately Mr Jaramillo, a committed Catholic, has been able to save some 350 children. Approximately 150 children still live in the sewers and the work of the Children of the Andes foundation continues unabated.

In spite of this heroic rescue of street children, it would surprise many to learn that Jaime appreciates the good life. He enjoys fine wine, eating out and dancing. He holidays in the Caribbean and Florida and when at home likes nothing better than sinking into his jacuzzi with a glass of brandy!

For further thought

1. Imagine you are a teenager living down a sewer. What might you write in your diary?
2. Essay: A day in the life of Jaime Jaramillo.
3. What is meant by the biblical term redemption? In what sense is Jaime an agent of redemption?

Source: *The Independent* (10th June 1991).

The Sicarios

Medellin, the Colombian city that has now become the drugs capital of the world, is not a place for anyone seeking to reach retirement age. Around five thousand people are murdered there every year.

Among its most deadly assassins are the sicarios – hired killers often still in their teens. La Plaga (Plague) is the boss of one of these gangs of killers. His attitude is blunt: 'You make a goal for yourself and go for it, and when you have a revolver in your hand you feel powerful. I started out helping my aunt who had a dope den selling drugs and vice. So I found myself taking the easy life.'

His sidekick, Freckles, killed his first victim when he was fourteen: 'I got real crazy when this guy hit me hard. So I got up right there. Bang . . . Bang . . . I plugged him in the crown with a .357 Magnum lent to me.'

Despite this behaviour the gang all claim to be practising Christians. They regularly visit a statue of the Virgin Mary to pray and light a candle before a hit. 'I go to church', says La Plague. 'Before a hit, I cross myself. It makes me calm.'

Peer pressure for these children is enormous: 'For me it's the money. You have to think about the money. After I killed someone I thought, hey, you can't kill people like that. That kid didn't do nothin' to me. He didn't hassle me. But you have to do it for the money,' laments Plague.

The local police force are tired of the sicarios, who regularly gun down their colleagues: 'A sicario is a man without a soul, a man without any moral limits. It's a delinquent of the worst kind,' comments Colonel Ferrero, a police official.

Yet film-maker Victor Gaviria is a little more sympathetic toward these young murderers: 'These kids have little opportunity in life. They are useless. So that even killing someone is a way to feel useful in society.'

Ultimately La Plaga sees little future for himself. Asked where he would end up, he replied: 'In a box, it could be any box, but it's always a box.'

For further thought

1. Who are the sicarios?
2. Why do the sicarios pray to the Virgin Mary before a 'hit'?
3. In what ways do the sicarios combine Christian and pagan beliefs?

Source: *YOU Magazine*, (24th March 1991).

CONCLUSION

Hope has been a major theme in our analysis of worldviews and religions. The Marxist, for example, places high hopes in the revolution which will abolish class struggle, exploitation and private property. The revolutionary has complete confidence in the power of science and technology to transform both man and society. The communist is motivated and inspired by this hope.

The Nazi, on the other hand, places his hope in the Führer and the eternal laws of natural selection. Inferior races and weak individuals will be eradicated in a wonderful world of tomorrow. There is hope for the world in the person of an Adolf Hitler.

Many eighteenth century intellectuals and scientists placed high hopes in the power of progress to usher in a perfect world. Many hippies of the 1960's believed in the power of LSD to redeem the world. The followers of Yellama believe that the practice of temple prostitution will guarantee abundant harvests.

In all this it is important to discern the intimate connection between belief and hope. *We could say that our deepest hopes reflect our deepest beliefs.* We have defined belief in terms of a disposition to live and behave in a certain way. Leopold and Loeb chose a way of life, including a squalid murder, that betrayed their deepest beliefs about the meaning and purpose of life. Exactly the same can be said for the lives of Hetty Green,

Elvis Presley, Imelda Marcos and Jaime Jaramillo. The lives of women and men reveal a tapestry of commitments, hopes and beliefs; this tapestry, although often unspoken and unacknowledged, can help us to understand the lives and deeds of all our friends and neighbours who live on this 'blue-green ball in black space' that we call earth.

It is impossible to avoid assumptions in any evaluation of a human life. When we are confronted with a Pol Pot or a Mother Theresa, we may choose to affirm, to condemn or simply to remain indifferent. We are always forced to respond to these lives whether good, bad or misled.

The two authors of this book are no different. We have chosen our point of commitment by which we judge and understand these wild, strange and compelling stories. We cannot and do not remain neutral. Our Christian faith cannot be hidden; our beliefs and commitments shape our understanding of men and women. Without doubt, we approve of some lives and disapprove of others. Three key biblical ideas undergird our analysis.

First, we believe and affirm that all people are created in God's image. All people, black, brown, yellow and white resemble God. This means that human beings bear the unmistakable value and dignity that God has bestowed upon the human race. Accordingly those who value human life primarily in terms of economic prosperity (I have killed you because you are poor and have no future) are fundamentally mistaken.

At the same time, the ethnic cleanser, indifferent to a person's economic standing, consumed by preoccupations of race and blood, is also fundamentally wrong.

For others it is physical beauty and the correct image that confer value upon a person; the ugly and the awkward are despised and rejected. This is equally flawed.

Second, we believe that idolatry dehumanises those people who are consumed and obsessed by false gods. Psalm 115 is illuminating:

Our God is in heaven:
he does whatever pleases him.
But their idols are silver and gold,
made by the hands of men.
They have mouths, but cannot speak,
eyes, but they cannot see;
they have ears, but cannot hear,
noses, but they cannot smell;
they have hands, but cannot feel,
feet, but they cannot walk;
nor can they utter a sound with their throats.
Those who make them will be like them,
and so will all who trust in them.

Psalm 115:3–8

If a person serves a false god, she or he will become like the false god that person loves. Hetty Green became so enamoured of her money that she lost all healthy and normal sensitivities. She sacrificed her personal hygiene, her comfort and ultimately her son's leg to her false absolute. Imelda Marcos became obsessed with her reputation and her image; she was willing to sacrifice countless lives in her quest for international recognition. And Earthfirst's eco-guerillas are willing to kill people in their defense of Mother Earth. In each case we encounter idolatry.

Idolatry always takes something that is good and then twists and destroys that good thing. For example it is good to be concerned with fashion and image; the two authors of this book are very attached to their 'trendy' leather jackets and would resist strongly the suggestion that they should exchange them for yellow anoraks! But such enjoyment of a good gift should never become obsessive. Our lives and values should never be ultimately guided and orchestrated by fashion, money or power. Such things are good but should never become sacred. This rich, biblical understanding of idolatry can help us to make sense of people's lives.

Third, we are called by God to place our hope and trust in Christ, the Messiah. It is foolish and ultimately fatal to believe that LSD or dead spirits can save us. It is equally misguided to believe in shopping or revolutionary fervour as ultimate 'fixers'.

Many people today have lost hope in traditional religions. Christianity can seem outdated and irrelevant. Many sophisticated westerners revel in their sceptical secularism, amused and bemused by the foolish pretensions of organised religion.

And yet there is a growing cynicism and disillusionment about the great slogans of atheism. Few today rhapsodise enthusiastically about the glories of science, progress and the classless society. In this mood of despair and exhausted secularism, some are returning to pre-Christian beliefs and hopes. There is a resurgence of interest in Celtic and Druidic beliefs; others are turning to witchcraft and the occult.

For some nihilism seems to be the only valid interpretation of life; life's a bitch and then you die! The morbid disposition of Kurt Cobain can appeal to some. At the same time, neo-fascism is growing in popularity in Europe; in the former Yugoslavia we are accustomed to hearing about 'ethnic cleansing'. In London, Nasreen, the unfortunate Pakistani girl, experiences fire bombs and racial taunts. In Russia we are witnessing the emergence of nationalism and xenophobia.

Paganism, occultism, nihilism and neo-fascism. Is this the poisonous cocktail that we are yet to enjoy?

Perhaps it is time to re-examine biblical hope. The nihilist is supremely pessimistic about the future; the Marxist is supremely optimistic. In a sense biblical hope cannot be referred to as either optimistic or pessimistic. Like nihilism, biblical hope fully appreciates the sordid and ravenous side of human nature; it does not eulogise about man's innate glory and goodness. At the same time the Bible acknowledges the dignity and value of human beings and points to an amazing future! A new heavens and a new earth, the home of righteousness. But this new world will not magically appear as the culmination of progress and human genius; rather God will usher in a new era with the return of Christ, the Messiah.

When enough is finally enough, the Christian confession assures us that Jesus Christ will return to judge the world and to restore all things (Acts 3:21). It is God and not man who will bring heaven to earth. But this hope in the future should never lead us to despair of the present. Like Jimmy Carter, Bob Lavelle and Jaime Jaramillo we must inject something of this amazing future into our world and into our lives today.

BIBLIOGRAPHY

General Introductions to Worldviews and Religions

Burnett, David. *Clash of Worlds*. Eastbourne: Monarch Publications, 1990.

Clouser, Roy. *The Myth of Religious Neutrality: An Essay on the Hidden Role of Religious Belief in Theories*. Notre Dame: University of Notre Dame Press, 1991.

Sire, James. *The Universe Next Door*. Downers Grove, Illinois: Inter-Varsity Press, 1976.

Smart, Ninian. *The World's Religions*. Cambridge: Cambridge University Press, 1989.

Walsh, Brian & Middleton, Richard. *The Transforming Vision: Shaping a Christian World View*. Downers Grove, Illinois: Inter-Varsity Press, 1984.

Wolters, Albert. *Creation Regained: Biblical Basics for a Reformational Worldview*. Leicester: Inter-Varsity Press, 1985.

Consumerism

Day, David & Husband, Tony. *True Tales of Environmental Madness*. London: Pelham Books, 1990.

Goudszwaard, Bob. *Capitalism and Progress: A Diagnosis of Western Society*. Translated by J. Van Nuis Zylstra. Grand Rapids, Michigan: Eerdmanns, 1979.

Lee-Wright, Peter. *Child Slaves*. London: Earthscan Publications, 1990.

Starkey, Mike. *Born to Shop: A Penetrating Look at the 'Loadsamoney' Culture*. Eastbourne: Monarch Publications, 1989.
Taylor, John. *Enough is Enough*. London: SCM, 1975.

Facism

Carr, W. Hitler: *A Study in Personality and Politics*. London: Edward Arnold, 1978.
Easlea, B. 'Psychotic Insecurity and Fascism.' in *Science and Sexual Oppression*. London: Weidenfeld and Nicolson, 1981.
Praamsma, L. *The Church in the Twentieth Century (Vol 7)* St. Catherines, Ontario, Canada: Paidea Press, 1981.

Communism

Hampsch, G. *The Theory of Communism*. New York: Citadel Press, 1965.
Marx, Karl & Engels, Friederich. *The Communist Manifesto*. Oxford: The World's Classics, 1992.
Stevenson, L. *Seven Theories of Human Nature*. Oxford: Oxford University Press, 1974.

Nihilism

Nietzsche, Friedrich. *Twilight of the Idols & The Anti-Christ*. Translated by R. J. Hollingdale. Harmondsworth, Middlesex: Penguin, 1968.
Sartre, Jean-Paul. *Being and Nothingness*. New York: Washington Square Press, 1966.
Schutte, Ofelia. *Beyond Nihilism: Nietzsche without Masks*. Chicago: Chicago University Press, 1984.
Russell, Bertrand. "A Free Man's Worship," in *Mysticism and Logic*. Watford: Taylor Garnett Evans & Co Ltd., 1910.

Eastern Religions

Anderson, J.N.D. *Christianity and World Religions*. Leicester: Inter-Varsity Press, 1984.

Hammer, Raymond. 'The Eternal Teaching: Hinduism' in *The World's Religions*. Tring: Lion Publishing plc, 1982.

Mascaro, Juan. 'Introduction to the Upanishads.' in *The Upanishads*. Translated by Juan Mascaro. Harmondsworth, Middlesex: Penguin Books, 1965.

Burnett, David, 'Gods and Gurus.' in *Clash of Worlds*. Eastbourne: Monarch Publications, 1990.

New Age

Groothius, Douglas R. *Unmasking the New Age*. Downers Grove, Illinois: Inter-Varsity Press, 1986.

Ferguson, Marilyn. *The Aquarian Conspiracy: Personal and Social Transformation in the 1980s*. Los Angeles: J.P. Tarcher, 1980.

Miller, Elliot. *A Crash Course on the New Age Movement*. Eastbourne: Monarch Publications, 1989.

Wilson, Stuart. *A Guide to the New Age*. Exeter, Devon: Wayseeker Books, 1989.

Islam

Burnett, David. 'Muhammad and the Message.' in *Clash of Worlds*. Eastbourne: Monarch Publications, 1990.

Musk, Bill A. *Passionate Believing: The 'Fundamentalist' Face of Islam*. Tunbridge Wells: Monarch Publications, 1992.

Musk, Bill A. *The Unseen Face of Islam*. Eastbourne: Monarch Publications, 1989.

Orphism and Gnosticism

Armstrong, A.H. *An Introduction to Ancient Philosophy*. Northampton: John Dickens & Co Ltd., 1947.

O'Grady, Joan, *Heresy*. Longmead, Dorset: Element Books Ltd., 1985.

Shaw, Steve. *No Splits*. London: Marshal Pickering, 1989.

Willard, Dallas. *The Spirit of the Disciplines*. New York: Harper-Collins, 1991.

Primal Religions

Burnett, David. *Unearthly Powers*. Eastbourne: Monarch Publications, 1988.

De Graaf, A. H. & Olthius, J. eds. *Kenya: A Way of Life*. Toronto: Curriculum Development Centre, 1981.

Rubingh, Eugene, *Sons of Tiv*. Grand Rapids: Baker Book House, 1969.

Turner, Harold W. *Living Tribal Religions*. London: Ward Lock Educational, 1974.

Paganism

Haining, Peter. *Superstitions*. London: Treasure Press, 1990.

MacCulloch, J. A. *The Religion of the Ancient Celts*. Edinburgh: Constable and Company Limited, 1911.

Perowne, Steward. *Roman Mythology*. London: Hamlyn Publishing Group Ltd., 1969.

Smith, Clyde Curry. 'The Ancient Religions of Greece and Rome.' in *The World Religions*. Tring: Lion, 1982.

Stewart, R. J. *The Waters of the Gap: Magic, Mythology and the Celtic Heritage*. Bath: Ashgrove Press, 1981.

Christianity

Campolo, Tony. *Wake Up America!* New York: HarperCollins, 1991.

Cooper, Tim. *Green Christianity: Caring for the Whole Creation.* London: Spire, 1990.

Craig, Mary. *Candles in the Dark: Six Modern Martyrs.* London: Hodder and Stoughton, 1984.

DeGraff, Arnold & Olthius, James, eds. *Towards a Biblical View of Man: Some Readings.* Toronto: Institute for Christian Studies, 1978.

De Graaf, S. G. *Promise and Deliverance* (Four Volumes) St. Catherines, Ontario, Canada: Paideia Press, 1977.

Kline, Meredith. *The Structure of Biblical Authority.* Grand Rapids, Michigan: Eerdmans, 1972.

Mouw, Richard. *When the Kings Come Marching In.* Grand Rapids, Mich: Eerdmans, 1984.

Seerveld, Calvin. *Balaam's Apocalyptic Prophecies: A Study in Reading Scripture.* Toronto: Wedge, 1980.

Sine, Tom. *The Mustard Seed Conspiracy.* London: MARC Europe, 1984.